Learn Java In One Day and Learn It Well
Java for Beginners with Hands-On Project
The only book you need to start coding in Java immediately

By Jamie Chan

http://www.learncodingfast.com/java

Preface

This book is written to help you learn Java FAST and learn it WELL.

The book does not assume any prior background in coding. If you are an absolute beginner, you'll find that this book explains complex concepts in an easy to understand manner. If you are an experienced coder but new to Java, this book will provide you with enough depth to start coding in Java immediately.

Topics are carefully selected to give you a broad exposure to Java, while not overwhelming you with information overload. These topics include object-oriented programming concepts, error handling techniques, file handling techniques and more. In addition, new features of Java such as lambda expressions are also covered. All examples in the book are carefully chosen to demonstrate each concept so that you can gain a deeper understanding of the language.

In addition, as Richard Branson puts it: "The best way of learning about anything is by doing". This book comes with a project where you'll be guided through the coding of a membership management software from scratch. The project uses concepts covered in the book and gives you a chance to see how it all ties together.

You can download the source code for the project and all the sample programs in this book at
http://www.learncodingfast.com/java

Contact Information

I would love to hear from you.
For feedback or queries, you can contact me at
jamie@learncodingfast.com.

More Books by Jamie

Python: Learn Python in One Day and Learn It Well (1st Edition)

Python: Learn Python in One Day and Learn It Well (2nd Edition)

C#: Learn C# in One Day and Learn It Well

SQL: Learn SQL (using MySQL) in One Day and Learn It Well

CSS: Learn CSS in One Day and Learn It Well

Table of Contents

Chapter 1: Introduction to Java

Welcome to Java programming and thank you so much for choosing my book among the large selection of Java books available.

Whether you are a seasoned programmer or a complete novice, this book is written to help you learn Java programming fast. Topics are carefully selected to give you a broad exposure to the fundamental concepts of Java while not overwhelming you with information overload. While it is not possible to cover every single Java concept in this book, rest assured that by the end of the book, you should have no problem writing your own Java programs. In fact, we will be coding a program together as part of the project at the end of the book. Ready to start?

Let's first answer a few questions:

1.1 What is Java?

Java is an object-oriented programming language developed by James Gosling at Sun Microsystems, which has since been acquired by Oracle Corporation. It was released in 1995 and is currently one of the most popular programming languages in use. It can be used to develop applications for a large variety of environments, such as applications for desktop, web and even mobile devices. One of the main features of Java is that it is platform independent. This means that a program written in Java can be executed on any operating system (such as Windows, Mac or Linux).

Like all modern programming languages, Java code resembles the English language which computers are unable to understand. Therefore, Java code has to be converted into machine code through a process known as compilation. Every computer platform has its own machine code instruction set. Hence, machine code that is compiled for one platform will not work on another platform. Most programming languages (like C and C++) compile written code into machine code directly. As a result, this machine code can only be run on the specific platform that the code is compiled for.

Java does it a little differently.

Instead of compiling into machine code directly, Java compiles all written code into bytecode first. Bytecode is platform independent. That is, there is no difference between the bytecode for Windows, Mac or Linux.

When a user wants to run a Java program, a program inside the user's computer (known as the Java Virtual Machine or JVM) converts this bytecode into machine code for the specific platform that the user uses.

The advantage of using this two-step compilation process is that it allows Java code to be run on all platforms as long as the computer running the Java program has JVM installed. JVM is free to download and there are different versions for different computer platforms. We'll learn how to install JVM in the next chapter.

1.2 Why Learn Java?

There are a lot of reasons why one should learn Java. Let's look at some of the reasons below.

Firstly, Java is currently one of the most popular programming languages in use. According to Oracle, 3 billion devices run Java. Furthermore, Android apps are also developed using Java. With the growing demand for mobile apps, it is safe to say that Java is an essential language to learn if you are interested in becoming a programmer.

Next, Java has syntax and features that resemble other programming languages like C and C++. If you have any prior programming experience, you will find learning Java a breeze. Even if you are totally new to programming, you can rest assured that Java is designed to be a relatively easy language to learn. Most programmers find it easier to learn Java than say, C or C++.

Java is also designed to be platform independent. As mentioned earlier, Java code is compiled into bytecode first, which can be run on any machine that has the Java Virtual Machine. Hence with Java, you can write the code once and run it anywhere you want.

Next, Java is an object-oriented programming (OOP) language. Object-oriented programming is an approach to programming that breaks a programming problem into objects that interact with each other. We'll be looking at various object-oriented programming concepts in this book. Once you master Java, you will be familiar with these concepts. This will make it easier for you to master other object-oriented programming languages in future.

Convinced that Java is a great language to learn? Let's move on.

Chapter 2: Getting Ready for Java

2.1 Installing JDK and NetBeans

Before we can start developing applications in Java, we need to download and install JDK and NetBeans. Both are free to download.

2.1.1 What is JDK?

JDK stands for Java Development Kit and is a free kit provided by Oracle that contains a number of tools to help us develop Java applications. Some of these tools include a compiler to compile our written code into bytecode (javac.exe), an archiver to package and distribute our Java files (jar.exe) and a documentation generator to generate HTML documentation from our Java code (javadoc.exe).

In addition, JDK also includes the Java Runtime Environment (JRE). JRE contains the JVM mentioned in Chapter 1 and the resources that JVM needs in order to run Java programs.

If you are only interested in running Java programs, all you need is the JRE. However, since we are also interested in developing Java programs, we need the JDK.

To download JDK, head over to https://www.oracle.com/java/technologies/javase-jdk11-downloads.html and scroll to the bottom of the page. You'll see a table with multiple download links. The version that you'll be downloading depends on the operating system that you are using. x86 and x64 refer to the 32-bit and 64-bit operating systems respectively. For instance, if you are using the 64-bit Windows operating system, you'll be downloading the "Windows-x64 Installer" exe file.

Once downloaded, double click on the downloaded file to install JDK.

2.1.2 What is NetBeans?

Besides JDK, we also need to install NetBeans.

NetBeans is an Integrated Development Environment (IDE) that we'll be using to facilitate our coding process. Strictly speaking, we can develop Java applications without using NetBeans. We can write our code in Notepad (or any other text editor) and compile and execute them using the tools provided in JDK. The screenshot below shows an example of how this can be done.

However, while it is possible to develop Java applications using the JDK alone, this process is tedious and error-prone.

To make coding easier, you are strongly encouraged to use an IDE. An IDE includes a text editor with advanced features for us to write our code, and provides us with a graphical user interface to debug, compile and run our applications. As we'll see later, these features will help greatly when coding. The IDE that we'll be using is NetBeans provided by Oracle.

To download NetBeans, head over to https://netbeans.apache.org/download/nb90/nb90.html. Scroll down to the "Downloading" section and click on the link for **Binaries** to download the file. Once downloaded, unzip the file onto your **Desktop**.

Once that is done, you are ready to start coding your first Java program.

2.2 How to use this book?

However, before we do that, I would like to highlight the fact that most of the code in Java consists of rather long statements. Hence, some statements may wrap around to the next line in this book. If you have problems reading the code samples, you can download the source code for all the sample programs at http://www.learncodingfast.com/java.

2.3 Your First Java Program

Now, let's start coding our first program.

First, navigate to the "netbeans\bin" folder in your unzipped Netbeans installation folder (located on your Desktop). For Windows users, depending on whether you are using a 32-bit or 64-bit Windows computer, double click on the *netbeans.exe* (for 32-bit computers) or *netbeans64.exe* (for 64-bit computers) file to launch Netbeans. For Mac users, double click on the *netbeans* file.

If you get an error message that says "Cannot find Java 1.8 or higher", you need to tell Netbeans where your JDK is installed.

For Windows users, JDK will likely be installed in *C:\Program Files\Java\jdk-****.

For Mac users, it will likely be installed in */Library/Java/JavaVirtualMachines/jdk-***.jdk/Contents/Home*.

In both cases, *** represents the version that you installed.

To tell Netbeans where JDK is installed, navigate to the "netbeans\etc" folder in your unzipped Netbeans installation folder. Open the *netbeans.conf* file with any text editor (e.g. Notepad) and use the "Find" function in your text editor to locate the line containing *netbeans_jdkhome*. If it is commented out (line starts with #), remove the # to uncomment it. Next, set the value of *netbeans_jdkhome* to the path of your JDK installation.

For instance, if JDK is installed in *C:\Program Files\Java\jdk-11.0.1*, you'll set *netbeans_jdkhome* as

```
netbeans_jdkhome="C:\Program Files\Java\jdk-11.0.1"
```

Once this is done, save and close the *netbeans.conf* file.

Launch Netbeans again. It should launch without error now.

If you are prompted to install the *nb-javac* library, you can go ahead and install it.

Next, select **File > New Project....** from the top menu bar.

You'll be prompted with the **New Project** dialog box. Select **Java** under *Categories* and **Java Application** under *Projects*. Click **Next** to continue.

On the next screen, name the project *HelloWorld* and take note of where the project is stored. Finally, click **Finish** to create the project.

You will be presented with a default template that NetBeans created for you automatically. Replace the code in the template with the code below.

Note that line numbers are added for reference and are not part of the actual code. You may want to bookmark this page for easy reference later when we discuss the program. You can also download the source code for this sample program and all other sample programs in this book at http://www.learncodingfast.com/java.

If you prefer not to type the whole program below, you can just delete all the lines with forward slash (/) and/or asterisk (*) on the left in the template and add lines 6 and 7 to it.

```
1 package helloworld;
2
3 public class HelloWorld {
4
5    public static void main(String[] args) {
6       //Print the words Hello World on the screen
7       System.out.println("Hello World");
8    }
9
10 }
```

However, I strongly encourage you to type the code yourself to get a better feel for how NetBeans works. As you type, you will notice some interesting features of NetBeans. For instance, you'll see that words are displayed in different colours. This is the software's way of making our code easier to read. Different words serve different purposes in our program and are thus displayed using different colours. We'll go into more details in later chapters.

In addition, you will also notice that a box appears near the cursor with some help messages occasionally. That is known as Intellisense. For instance, when you type a period (.) after the word System, a dropdrop list appears to let you know what you can type after the period, with a box that provides further information.

Finally, also note that NetBeans will automatically close brackets for you when you type an opening bracket. For instance, when you type "(", NetBeans will add the closing bracket ")" for you.

These are some of the features that NetBeans provides to make coding easier for us.

After you finish typing, save the program by selecting **File > Save**. NetBeans has a "Compile on Save" feature that compiles the code whenever you save it. You can then execute the compiled program by clicking on the **Run** button at the top menu (refer to image below).

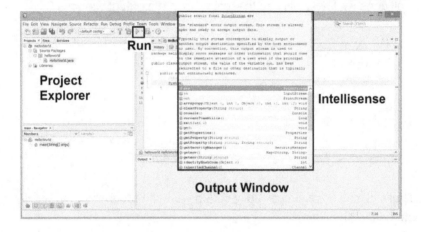

If your program fails to run, there will be a pop up box with an error message. Click **Run Anyway** to continue. You will then see a description of the error in the output window (refer to next image). Alternatively, you can also hover your mouse over the red squiggly line in the text editor window. That will provide you with another clue about what went wrong. Try to identify and correct the mistake and run the program again.

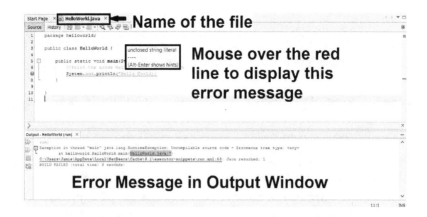

Name of the file

Mouse over the red line to display this error message

Error Message in Output Window

If all goes well, you will see the following in the output window.

```
run:
Hello World
BUILD SUCCESSFUL (total time: 0 seconds)
```

This program simply displays the words "Hello World" in the output window. The other two sentences are additional information provided by NetBeans and are not part of our program output.

That's it! You have successfully coded your first program. Give yourself a pat on the shoulders.

The name of the Java file that you just wrote is *HelloWorld.java*. You can find the name at the top of the text editor window (refer to image above).

2.4 Basic Structure of a Java Program

Now, let us do a quick run-through of the basic program that you just coded.

2.4.1 Package

On the first line, we have the statement

```
package helloworld;
```

This statement tells the compiler that the Java file we wrote belongs to the `helloworld` package.

A package is simply a grouping of related classes and interfaces. Do not worry if you do not know what classes and interfaces are, we'll cover them in subsequent chapters.

When we write `package helloworld;` at the top of our file, we are asking the compiler to include this file in the `helloworld` package. The compiler will then create a folder named "helloworld" and save the file into that folder. Files that belong to the same package are stored in the same folder.

If you navigate to your "NetBeansProjects" folder now, you'll find a folder named "HelloWorld". The "NetBeansProject" folder is normally located in your "Documents" folder. If you can't find this folder, try searching for it using your computer's search function.

Within the "HelloWorld" folder, you'll find a "src" folder that contains the "helloworld" folder.

This folder stores the files of the `helloworld` package. It is a convention for us to name our packages in lowercase. Note that Java is a case-sensitive language. Hence, "HelloWorld" is not the same as "helloworld". Inside the "helloworld" folder, you'll find the *HelloWorld.java* file.

The advantage of declaring packages is that it prevents naming conflicts. Two or more files can have the same name as long as they belong to different packages. This is similar to how you can have two or more files of the same name on your computer as long as you put them in different folders. We'll learn how to create different packages in Chapter 8.

In addition to packages created by us, Java also comes with a large number of pre-created packages that contain code that we can use in our programs. For instance, code for input and output is bundled in the java.io package while code for implementing the components of a graphical user interface (like buttons, menus, etc) is bundled in the `java.awt` package. To use these pre-written packages, we need to import them into our programs. We'll learn how to do that at a later time.

2.4.2 The HelloWorld Class

Next, let's move on to the `HelloWorld` class. We'll talk more about classes in Chapter 7. For now, just know that in our example, the `HelloWorld` class starts on line 3 with an opening curly brace and ends on line 10 with a closing curly brace. Curly braces are used extensively in Java to indicate the start and end of a code element. All opening braces in Java must be closed with a corresponding closing brace.

Within the `HelloWorld` class, we have the `main()` method which starts on line 5 and ends on line 8.

2.4.3 The main() Method

The `main()` method is the entry point of all Java applications. Whenever a Java application is started, the `main()` method is the first method to be called.

Notice the words `String[] args` inside the parenthesis of our `main()` method? This means the `main()` method can take in an array of strings as input. Do not worry about this for the moment. We'll cover arrays and input in subsequent chapters.

In our example, the `main()` method contains two lines of code. The first line

```
//Print the words Hello World on the screen
```

is known as a comment and is ignored by the compiler.

The second line

```
System.out.println("Hello World");
```

displays the line "Hello World" (without quotes) on the output window (located at the bottom of the screen). Note that this statement ends with a semi-colon. All statements in Java must end with a semi-colon (;). This is similar to most of the other programming languages like C and C++.

After the `System.out.println("Hello World");` statement, we end our code with two closing braces to close the earlier opening braces. That's it! There's all there is to this simple program.

2.5 Comments

We've covered quite a bit in this chapter. You should now have a basic understanding of Java programming and be reasonably comfortable with NetBeans. Before we end this chapter, there's one more thing to learn - comments.

We mentioned in the previous section that the line

```
//Print the words Hello World on the screen
```

is a comment and is ignored by the compiler.

A comment is actually not part of the program. It is added to our code to make it more readable for other programmers. As such, comments are not compiled into bytecode.

To add comments to our program, we type two forward slashes (//) in front of each line of comment like this

```
// This is a comment
// This is another comment
// This is yet another comment
```

Alternatively, we can also use /* ... */ for multiline comments like this

```
/* This is a comment
This is also a comment
This is yet another comment
*/
```

Comments can also be placed after a statement, like this:

```
System.out.println("Hello");  //prints the word Hello
```

Chapter 3: The World of Variables and Operators

Now that you are familiar with NetBeans and have some basic understanding of a Java program, let's get down to the real stuff. In this chapter, you'll learn all about variables and operators. Specifically, you'll learn what variables are and how to name, declare and initialize them. You'll also learn about the common operations that we can perform on them.

3.1 What are variables?

Variables are names given to data that we need to store and manipulate in our programs. For instance, suppose your program needs to store the age of a user. To do that, we can name this data `userAge` and declare the variable `userAge` using the following statement:

```
int userAge;
```

This declaration statement first states the data type of the variable, followed by its name. The data type of a variable refers to the type of data that the variable will store (such as whether it's a number or a piece of text). In our example, the data type is `int`, which refers to integers. The name of our variable is `userAge`.

After you declare the variable `userAge`, your program will allocate a certain area of your computer's memory space to store this data. You can then access and modify this data by referring to it by its name, `userAge`.

3.2 Primitive Data Types in Java

There are eight basic data types that are predefined in Java. These are known as primitive data types.

The first 4 data types are for storing integers (i.e. numbers with no fractional parts). They are as follows:

byte

The `byte` data type is used for storing integers from -128 to 127. It uses 1 byte of storage space (this is known as the width or the size of the data type). We normally use the `byte` data type if storage space is a concern or if we are certain the value of the variable will not exceed the -128 to 127 range.

For instance, we can use the `byte` data type to store the age of a user as it is unlikely that the user's age will ever exceed 127 years old.

short

The `short` data type uses 2 bytes of storage space and has a range of -32768 to 32767.

int

The `int` data type uses 4 bytes of storage space and has a range of -2^{31} (-2147483648) to $2^{31}-1$ (2147483647). It is the most commonly used data type for storing integers as it has the most practical range.

long

The `long` data type uses 8 bytes of storage space and has a range of -2^{63} to $2^{63}-1$. It is rarely used unless you really need to store a very large integer (such as the number of inhabitants on Earth). In order to specify a long value, you have to add the suffix "L" to the end of the number. We'll talk more about suffixes in the next section.

In addition to having data types for storing integers, we also have data types for storing floating point numbers (i.e. numbers with fractional parts). They are:

float

The `float` data type uses 4 bytes of storage and has a range of approximately negative $3.40282347 \times 10^{38}$ to positive $3.40282347 \times 10^{38}$. It has a precision of about 7 digits. This means that if you use `float` to store a number like 1.23456789 (10 digits), the number will be rounded off to approximately 7 digits (i.e. 1.234568).

double

The `double` data type uses 8 bytes of storage and has a range of approximately negative $1.79769313486231570 \times 10^{308}$ to positive $1.79769313486231570 \times 10^{308}$, with a precision of approximately 15 digits.

By default, whenever you specify a floating point number in Java, it is automatically considered to be a `double`, not a `float`. If you want Java to treat the floating point number as a `float`, you have to add a suffix "F" to the end of the number.

Unless memory space is a concern, you should always use a `double` instead of a `float` as it is more precise.

Besides the six data types mentioned above, Java has two more primitive data types. They are:

char

`char` stands for character and is used to store single Unicode characters such as 'A', '%', '@' and 'p' etc. It uses 2 bytes of memory.

boolean

`boolean` is a special data type that can only hold two values: `true` and `false`. It is commonly used in control flow statements. We'll cover control flow statements in Chapter 6.

3.3 Naming a Variable

A variable name in Java can only contain letters, numbers, underscores (_) or the dollar sign ($). However, the first character cannot be a number. Hence, you can name your variables `_userName`, `$username`, `username` or `userName2` but not `2userName`.

The convention, however, is to always begin your variable names with a letter, not "$" or "_". Additionally, the dollar sign character is almost never used when naming a variable (although it is not technically wrong to use it).

Variable names should be short but meaningful, designed to indicate to the casual reader the intent of its use. It makes more sense to name your variables `userName`, `userAge` and `userNumber`, instead of `n`, `a` and `un`.

In addition, there are some reserved words that you cannot use as a variable name because they already have pre-assigned meanings in Java. These reserved words include words like `System`, `if`, `while` etc. We'll learn about each of them in subsequent chapters.

It is common practice to use camel casing when naming variables in Java. Camel casing is the practice of writing compound words with mixed casing, capitalising the first letter of each word except the first word (e.g. `thisIsAVariableName`). This is the convention that we'll be using in the rest of the book.

Finally, variable names are case sensitive. `thisIsAVariableName` is not the same as `thisisavariablename`.

3.4 Initializing a Variable

Every time you declare a new variable, you need to give it an initial value. This is known as initializing the variable. You can change the value of the variable in your program later.

There are two ways to initialize a variable. You can initialize it at the point of declaration or initialize it in a separate statement.

The code below shows how you can initialize variables at the point of declaration (line numbers on the left are added for reference and are not part of the code).

```
1  byte userAge = 20;
2  short numberOfStudents = 45;
3  int numberOfEmployees = 500;
4  long numberOfInhabitants = 21021313012678L;
5
6  float hourlyRate = 60.5F;
7  double numberOfHours = 5120.5;
8
9  char grade = 'A';
10 boolean promote = true;
11
12 byte level = 2, userExperience = 5;
```

As mentioned above, in order to specify a long value, you have to add the suffix "L" to the end of the number. Hence, on line 4 when we initialized numberOfInhabitants, we added "L" to the end of the number. If we do not do that, the compiler will complain that the number is too large and give us an error.

In addition, when we initialized the variable hourlyRate on line 6, we added the suffix "F". This is because by default, any floating point number is treated as a double by Java. We need to add the suffix "F" to indicate to the compiler that hourlyRate is of float data type.

Finally, when initializing a char data type, we need to enclose the character in single quotes as shown on line 9.

On line 12, we see an example of how you can declare and initialize two variables of the same data type in one statement. The two variables are separated by a comma, and there is no need to state the data type of the second variable.

The examples above show how you can initialize a variable at the point of declaration. Alternatively, you can choose to declare and initialize a variable in two separate statements as shown below:

```
byte year;    //declare the variable first
year = 20;    //initialize it later
```

3.5 The Assignment Operator

The = sign in programming has a different meaning from the = sign we learned in Math. In programming, the = sign is known as an assignment operator. It means we are assigning the value on the right side of the = sign to the variable on the left.

In programming, the statements $x = y$ and $y = x$ have very different meanings.

Confused? An example will likely clear this up.

Suppose we declare two variables x and y as follows:

```
int x = 5;
int y = 10;
```

If you write

```
x = y;
```

your Math teacher is probably going to be upset at you since x is not equal to y. However, in programming, this is fine.

This statement means we are assigning the value of y to x. It is alright to assign the value of a variable to another variable. In our example, the value of x is now changed to 10 while the value of y remains unchanged. In other words, $x = 10$ and $y = 10$ now.

If we now change the values of x and y to 3 and 20 respectively by writing

```
x = 3;
y = 20;
```

and write

```
y = x;
```

we are assigning the value of x to the variable y. Hence, y becomes 3 while the value of x remains unchanged (i.e. $y = 3$, $x = 3$ now).

3.6 Basic Operators

Besides assigning an initial value to a variable or assigning another variable to it, we can also perform the usual mathematical operations on variables. Basic operators in Java include $+$, $-$, $*$, $/$ and $\%$ which represent addition, subtraction, multiplication, division and modulus respectively.

Example

Suppose x = 7, y = 2

Addition:	x + y = 9
Subtraction:	x - y = 5
Multiplication:	x*y = 14
Division:	x/y = 3 (rounds down the answer to the nearest integer)
Modulus:	x%y = 1 (gives the remainder when 7 is divided by 2)

In Java, division gives an integer answer if both x and y are integers. However, if either x or y is a non integer, we will get a non integer answer. For instance,

$7 / 2 = 3$
$7.0 / 2 = 3.5$
$7 / 2.0 = 3.5$
$7.0 / 2.0 = 3.5$

In the first case, when an integer is divided by another integer, you get an integer as the answer. The decimal portion of the answer, if any, is truncated. Hence, we get 3 instead of 3.5.

In all other cases, the result is a non integer as at least one of the operands is a non integer.

Note that 7.0 is not the same as 7 in Java. The former is a floating point number while the latter is an integer.

3.7 More Assignment Operators

Besides the $=$ operator, there are a few more assignment operators in Java (and most programming languages). These include operators like +=, -= and *=.

Suppose we have the variable x, with an initial value of 10. If we want to increment x by 2, we can write

```
x = x + 2;
```

The program will first evaluate the expression on the right ($x + 2$) and assign the answer to the left. So eventually x becomes 12.

Instead of writing $x = x + 2$, we can also write $x += 2$ to express the same meaning. The += operator is a shorthand that combines the assignment operator with the addition operator. Hence, `x += 2` simply means `x = x + 2`.

Similarly, if we want to do a subtraction, we can write `x = x - 2` or `x - = 2`. The same works for all the 5 operators mentioned in the section above.

Most programming languages also have the `++` and `--` operators. The `++` operator is used when you want to increase the value of a variable by 1. For instance, suppose

```
int x = 2;
```

If you write

```
x++;
```

the value of `x` becomes 3.

There is no need to use the `=` operator when you use the `++` operator. The statement `x++;` is equivalent to

```
x = x + 1;
```

The `++` operator can be placed in front of or behind the variable name. This affects the order in which tasks are performed.

Suppose we have an integer named `counter`. If we write

```
System.out.println(counter++);
```

the program first prints the original value of `counter` before incrementing `counter` by 1. In other words, it executes the tasks in this order

```
System.out.println(counter);
counter = counter + 1;
```

On the other hand, if we write

```
System.out.println(++counter);
```

the program first increments `counter` by 1 before printing the new value of `counter`. In other words, it executes the tasks in this order

```
counter = counter + 1;
System.out.println(counter);
```

In addition to the `++` operator, we also have the `--` operator (two minus signs). This operator decreases the value of the variable by 1.

3.8 Type Casting In Java

Sometimes in our program, it is necessary to convert from one data type to another, such as from a `double` to an `int`. This is known as type casting.

If we want to convert a smaller data type into a larger data type, we do not need to do anything explicitly. For instance, the code below assigns a `short` (2 bytes) to a `double` (8 bytes). This is known as a widening primitive conversion and does not require any special code on our part.

```
short age = 10;
double myDouble = age;
```

However, if we want to assign a larger data type to a smaller data type, we need to indicate it explicitly using a pair of parenthesis. This is known as a narrowing primitive conversion. The example below shows how it can be done.

```
int x = (int) 20.9;
```

Here, we can casting a `double` (8 bytes) into an `int` (4 bytes).

Narrowing conversion is not safe and should be avoided unless absolutely necessary. This is because narrowing conversion can result in a loss of data. When we cast 20.9 into an `int`, the resulting value is 20, not 21. The decimal portion is truncated after the conversion.

We can also cast a `double` into a `float`. Recall that we mentioned earlier that all non integers are treated as `double` by default in Java? If we want to assign a number like 20.9 to a float, we need to add a suffix 'F' to the number. Another way to do it is to use a cast, like this:

```
float num1 = (float) 20.9;
```

The value of `num1` will be 20.9.

In addition to casting between numeric types, we can also do other types of casting. We'll explore some of these conversions in subsequent chapters.

Chapter 4: Arrays and Strings

In the previous chapter, we covered the eight primitive data types in Java. Besides these primitive types, Java also comes with a few advanced data types. In this chapter, we are going to cover two of them: strings and arrays. In addition, we are going to discuss the difference between a primitive data type and a reference data type.

4.1 String

First, let us look at strings. A string is essentially a piece of text such as "Hello World" or "Good morning".

To declare and initialize a `String` variable, you write

```
String message = "Hello World";
```

where `message` is the name of the `String` variable and "Hello World" is the string assigned to it. Note that you need to enclose the string in double quotes (").

You can also assign an empty string to a `String` variable like this:

```
String anotherMessage = "";
```

If you want to join two or more strings together, you can use the concatenate sign (+). For instance, you can write

```
String myName = "Hello World, " + "my name is Jamie";
```

This is the same as

```
String myName = "Hello World, my name is Jamie";
```

String disadvantage = unchangable

when we are updating a string variable

4.1.1 String Methods

Unlike the 8 primitive types we looked at in the previous chapter, a `String` is actually an object. Specifically, it is an object of the `String` class.

Do not worry if you don't understand what this means; we'll discuss classes and objects in Chapter 7. For now, all that you have to know is that the `String` class provides us with a number of pre-written methods that we can use when working with strings. A method is a block of reusable code that performs a certain task. We'll look at some examples later.

In Java, a method may have different variations. Most of the examples below discuss only one of the variations for each method. However, if you learn how to use one variation, you can figure out how to use the other variations with relative ease. Let's look at some of the commonly used `String` methods now.

length()

The `length()` method tells us the total number of characters the string has.

To find the length of the string "Hello World", we write

```
"Hello World".length();
```

Whenever we use a method, we need to use the dot operator. We type the name of the method (`length` in this case) after the dot operator, followed by a pair of parenthesis (). Most methods return an answer after they complete their tasks. The `length()` method returns the length of the string. You can assign this result to a variable as shown below.

```
int myLength = "Hello World".length();
```

every time we are using new keyword we are allocating a memory (we are creating new ----)

In the example above, `myLength` will be equal to 11 as "Hello" and "World" both have 5 characters each. When you add the space between the two words, you get a total length of 11.

You can display the result of the `length()` method using the statements below.

```
int myLength = "Hello World".length();
System.out.println(myLength);
```

Try adding the two statements above to the *HelloWorld.java* file you wrote earlier in Chapter 2. You'll have to add them inside the opening and closing braces of the `main()` method. Run the program. You'll see the value 11 displayed as the output. We'll talk more about displaying outputs in the next chapter.

toUpperCase()/toLowerCase()

The `toUpperCase()` method is used to convert a string to uppercase characters. The `toLowerCase()` method is used to convert a string to lowercase characters.

For instance, to change the string "Hello World" to upper case, we can write

```
String uCase = "Hello World".toUpperCase();
```

On the right side of the statement, we use the string "Hello World" to call the `toUpperCase()` method. We then assign the result to the variable `uCase`.

`uCase` will thus be equal to "HELLO WORLD".

substring()

The `substring()` method is used to extract a substring from a longer string.

Some methods in Java require certain data for them to work. These data are known as arguments. We include these arguments in the pair of parenthesis that follows the method name. The `substring()` method is an example of a method that requires one argument to work.

For instance, to extract a substring from "Hello World", we can use the statement below:

```
String firstSubstring = "Hello World".substring(6);
```

On the right side of the statement, we use the "Hello World" string to call the `substring()` method. The number 6 in the parenthesis is known as the argument. This argument tells the compiler where to start extracting the substring. Essentially, it is asking the compiler to extract the substring starting from index 6 (i.e. position 6) to the end of the string.

Note that in programming, index starts with a value of ZERO not 1. This is a common practice in almost all programming languages such as Python and Java. Hence, in our example, 'H' is at index 0 while 'W' is at index 6.

The statement above will extract the substring "World". This result is then assigned to `firstSubstring`.

`firstSubstring` is thus equal to "World".

The `substring()` method also comes with another variation that allows us to extract a substring from one index to another. Suppose you want to extract a substring from position 1 to 7, you can do it as follows:

```
String message = "Hello World";
String secondSubstring = message.substring(1, 8);
```

In the example above, we first assigned "Hello World" to the variable `message`. We then use `message` to call the `substring()` method.

The two arguments are 1 and 8.

As before, the first argument tells the compiler the index of the starting position to extract. The second argument tells the compiler the index of the first position to stop extracting. In other words, in our example, the compiler stops extracting **at** position 8 (not after position 8). That means the letter at position 8 is not included in the substring. Hence, the substring extracted is "ello Wo".

`secondSubstring` is thus equal to "ello Wo".
`message` remains as "Hello World".

charAt()

The `charAt()` method returns a single character at a specified location. This character can then be assigned to a `char` variable.

For instance, the statement

```
char myChar = "Hello World".charAt(1);
```

extracts the character at index 1 and assigns it to `myChar`. Hence, `myChar` is equal to 'e'.

equals()

The `equals()` method is used to compare if two strings are identical. It returns `true` if the strings are equal and `false` if they are not.

If we have the statements:

```
boolean equalsOrNot = "This is Jamie".equals("This is Jamie");
boolean equalsOrNot2 = "This is Jamie".equals("Hello World");
```

`equalsOrNot` will be `true` while `equalsOrNot2` will be `false`.

split()

The `split()` method splits a string into substrings based on a user-defined separator (also known as a delimiter). After splitting the string, the `split()` method returns an array that contains the resulting substrings. An array is a collection of related data. We'll discuss arrays in the next section.

Suppose you want to split the string "Peter, John, Andy, David" into substrings, you can do it as follows:

```
String names = "Peter, John, Andy, David";
String[] splitNames = names.split(", ");
```

Here, we first assign the string that we want to split to the variable names. We then use `names` to call the `split()` method. The `split()` method takes in one argument – the delimiter used to separate the substring. In our example, the delimiter is a comma followed by a space.

The result of the code above is the following array
```
{"Peter", "John", "Andy", "David"}
```

This array is assigned to the variable `splitNames`.

We've covered a number of the commonly used `String` methods in Java. For a complete list of all the `String` methods available, check out this page https://docs.oracle.com/javase/8/docs/api/java/lang/String.html#method.summary.

4.2 Array

Next, let us look at arrays.

An array is a collection of data that are normally related to each other. Suppose we want to store the ages of 5 users. Instead of storing them as `user1Age`, `user2Age`, `user3Age`, `user4Age` and `user5Age`, we can store them as an array.

There are two ways to declare an array variable. The first way is to declare it as follows:

```
int[] userAge;
```

`int` indicates that this variable stores `int` values.
`[]` indicates that the variable is an array instead of a normal variable.
`userAge` is the name of the array.

The second way to declare it is as follows:

```
int userAge[];
```

This style comes from the C/C++ language and was adopted in Java to accommodate C/C++ programmers. However, this is not the preferred syntax in Java. We'll stick to the first style in this book.

After you declare an array variable, you need to create an array and assign it to the variable. To do that, we use the `new` keyword as shown below:

```
int[] userAge;
userAge = new int[] {21, 22, 23; 24, 25};
```

The first statement declares the array variable `userAge`. The second statement creates the array {`21, 22, 23, 24 and 25`} and assigns it to `userAge`. Since `userAge` has not been assigned any array previously, this statement initializes `userAge` with the created array. Once you initialize an array, the size of the array cannot be changed anymore. In this case, the array `userAge` can only hold 5 values from now onwards as we initialized it with 5 integers. {`21, 22, 23, 24, 25`} are the five integers that the array stores currently.

In addition to declaring and initializing an array in two statements, we can combine the two statements into a single statement using the shortcut syntax below:

```
int[] userAge2 = new int[] {21, 22, 23, 24, 25};
```

We can further simplify this statement to

```
int[] userAge2 = {21, 22, 23, 24, 25};
```

That is, you can omit the words `new int[]` if you declare and initialize an array in the same statement.

A third way to declare and initialize an array is as follows:

```
int[] userAge3 = new int[5];
```

This statement declares an array `userAge3` and initializes it with an array of 5 integers (as indicated by the number 5 inside the square brackets [ ]). As we did not specify the values of these 5 integers, Java automatically creates an array using the default value and assigns it to `userAge3`. The default value for integers is 0. Hence, `userAge3` becomes `{0, 0, 0, 0, 0}`.

You can update the individual elements in the array by accessing them using their indexes. Recall that indexes always start with a value of zero. The first element of the array has an index of 0, the next has an index of 1 and so forth. Suppose the array `userAge` is currently `{21, 22, 23, 24, 25}`. To update the first element of the array, we write

```
userAge[0] = 31;
```

the array becomes `{31, 22, 23, 24, 25}`.

If we type

```
userAge[2] = userAge[2] + 20;
```

the array becomes {31, 22, 43, 24, 25}. That is, 20 is added to the third element.

[handwritten: Array — non-primitive and reference data type]

4.2.1 Array Methods

Like strings, arrays also come with a number of pre-written methods.

The methods that we discuss below are found in the `java.util.Arrays` class. To use them, you have to add the statement

```
import java.util.Arrays;
```

to your program. This is to tell the compiler where to find the code for these methods.

The import statement must appear after the package statement and before the class declaration. An example is shown below:

```
package helloworld;

import java.util.Arrays;

public class HelloWorld {

      //Code for HelloWorld class
}
```

[handwritten: Simple variable hold multiple same types]

You may recall that previously when we used the `String` class, we did not have to write any import statement. This is because the `String` class is present in the `java.lang package` which is imported by default in all Java programs.

Now, let us look at some of the commonly used methods for arrays.

[handwritten: Non primitive = holding address in memory]
[handwritten: Primitive = holding actual value]

Index number start from zero

equals()

The equals () method is used to determine if two arrays are equal to each other. It returns true if the arrays are equal and false if they are not. Two arrays are considered equal if they have the same number of elements and the elements are arranged in the same order.

Suppose you have the following code segment:

```
int[] arr1 = {0,2,4,6,8,10};
int[] arr2 = {0,2,4,6,8,10};
int[] arr3 = {10,8,6,4,2,0};

boolean result1 = Arrays.equals(arr1, arr2);
boolean result2 = Arrays.equals(arr1, arr3);
```

result1 will be true while result2 will be false. This is because for result2, even though arr1 and arr3 have the same elements, the elements are not arranged in the same order. Hence, the two arrays are not considered equal.

Note that in the example above, we added the word Arrays in front of the method name. This is because all methods in the Arrays class are static. To call a static method, you have to add the name of the class in front. We'll talk more about static methods in Chapter 7.

copyOfRange()

The copyOfRange () method allows you to copy the contents of one array into another. It requires three arguments.

Suppose you have

```
int [] source = {12, 1, 5, -2, 16, 14, 18, 20, 25};
```

You can copy the contents of source into a new array dest using the statement below:

```
int[] dest = Arrays.copyOfRange(source, 3, 7);
```

The first argument (`source`) is the array that provides the values to be copied. The second and third arguments tell the compiler at which index to start and stop copying respectively. In other words, in our example, we are copying elements from index 3 to index 6 (i.e. the element at index 7 is not copied).

After copying the elements, the `copyOfRange()` method returns an array with the numbers copied. This array is then assigned to `dest`.

Hence, `dest` becomes {-2, 16, 14, 18} while `source` remains unchanged.

toString()

The `toString()` method returns a `String` that represents the contents of an array. This makes it easy for us to display the contents of the array. For instance, suppose you have

```
int[] numbers = {1, 2, 3, 4, 5};
```

You can use the statement below to display the contents of `numbers`.

```
System.out.println(Arrays.toString(numbers));
```

You will get

```
[1, 2, 3, 4, 5]
```

as the output.

sort()

The `sort()` method allows us to sort our arrays. It takes in an array as the argument.

Suppose you have

```
int [] numbers2 = {12, 1, 5, -2, 16, 14};
```

You can sort this array by writing

```
Arrays.sort(numbers2);
```

The array will be sorted in ascending order.

The `sort()` method does not return a new array. It simply modifies the array that is passed in. In other words, it modifies the `numbers2` array in our example. You can then use the statement

```
System.out.println(Arrays.toString(numbers2));
```

to print out the sorted array. You will get

```
[-2, 1, 5, 12, 14, 16]
```

as the output.

binarySearch()

The `binarySearch()` method allows you to search for a specific value in a sorted array. To use this method, make sure your array is sorted first. You can use the `sort()` method mentioned above to do so.

Suppose we have the following array:

```
int[] myInt = {21, 23, 34, 45, 56, 78, 99};
```

To determine if 78 is inside the array, we write

```
int foundIndex = Arrays.binarySearch(myInt, 78);
```

`foundIndex` will be equal to 5. This indicates that the number 78 is found at index 5.

On the other hand, if you write

```
int foundIndex2 = Arrays.binarySearch(myInt, 39);
```

`foundIndex2` will be equal to -4.

There are two parts to this result – the negative sign and the number 4.

The negative sign simply indicates that 39 is not found.

The number 4, on the other hand, is kind of weird. It tells you where the number should be if it exists in the array. However, it adds ONE to that index. In other words, if the number 39 exists in the array, it should be at index 4-1 = 3.

We've covered some of the more commonly used array methods in this section. For a complete list of all the array methods available in Java, check out this page
https://docs.oracle.com/javase/8/docs/api/java/util/Arrays.html

4.2.2 Finding Array Length

Finally, let's look at how we can find the length of an array. The length of an array tells us the number of items the array has. Previously when we discussed strings, we mentioned we can use the `length()` method to find the length of a string.

Contrary to what most would believe, there is no `length()` method when working with arrays. Instead, to find the length of an array, we use the `length` field. We'll talk about fields vs methods in Chapter 7. For now, all you have to know is that to find the length of an array, you do not need to add parenthesis after the word `length`.

For instance, if we have

```
int [] userAge = {21, 22, 26, 32, 40};
```

`userAge.length` is equal to 5 as there are 5 numbers in the array.

4.3 Primitive Type vs. Reference Type

Now that we are familiar with strings and arrays, let us discuss an important concept regarding data types in Java.

All data types in Java can be classified as either a primitive type or a reference type. There are only 8 primitive types in Java (`byte`, `short`, `int`, `long`, `float`, `double`, `char` and `boolean`), the rest are reference types. Examples of reference types include strings and arrays discussed in this chapter, and classes and interfaces that will be discussed in Chapter 7 and 8.

One of the main differences between a primitive type and a reference type is the data that is stored.

A primitive type stores its own data.

When we write

```
int myNumber = 5;
```

the variable `myNumber` stores the actual value 5.

A reference type, on the other hand, does not store the actual data. Instead, it stores a reference to the data. It does not tell the compiler what the value of the data is; it tells the compiler where to find the actual data.

An example of a reference type is a `String`. When you write a statement like

```
String message = "Hello";
```

the variable `message` actually does not store the string "Hello".

Instead, the string "Hello" is created and stored elsewhere in the computer's memory. The variable `message` stores the address of that memory location.

That's all that we need to know about reference types at the moment. As this is a book for beginners, we will not go into details about why reference types are necessary. Just be aware that there is a difference between primitive types and reference types; the former stores a value while the latter stores an address.

4.4 Strings are Immutable

Before I end this chapter, I would like to cover one more concept about strings. Specifically, I would like to point out that strings are immutable in Java (and most other languages).

Immutable means the value of a string cannot be changed. Whenever we update a `String` variable, we are actually creating a new string and assigning the memory address to the `String` variable. Let's consider an example. Suppose we have

```
String message = "Hello";
```

We learned earlier that the compiler will create the string "Hello" and store it somewhere in the computer's memory. The variable `message` stores the address of that location. Now, if we update the value of `message` to "World" as shown below

```
message = "World";
```

the compiler actually does not go to the location where "Hello" is stored to change its value to "World". Instead, it creates a new string "World" and stores it somewhere else in the computer's memory. This new address is then assigned to `message`. In other words, there are two strings now: "Hello" and "World". `message` stores the address of "World". If "Hello" is no longer needed in the program, it is eventually destroyed so as to free up that memory location. This process is known as garbage collection and is handled automatically by Java.

Chapter 5: Making our Program Interactive

Now that we have covered the basics of variables and data types, let us write a program that accepts input from users, stores the data in a variable and displays messages to our users. After all, what good is a computer program if it cannot interact with its users?

5.1 Displaying Output

We've already seen some examples of displaying outputs to users in Chapter 2 and 4.

Simply stated, to display outputs to our users, we can use the `print()` or `println()` method provided by Java. In order to use these methods, we have to add `System.out` in front of the method names. This is because the two methods belong to the `PrintStream` class and we have to use `System.out` to access them. Do not worry if this sounds very confusing at the moment. We'll learn more about classes and methods in Chapter 7.

The difference between the `println()` and `print()` methods is that `println()` moves the cursor down to the next line after displaying the message while `print()` does not.

For instance, if we write

```
System.out.println("Hello ");
System.out.println ("How are you?");
```

we'll get

```
Hello
How are you?
```

If we write

```
System.out.print("Hello ");
System.out.print("How are you?");
```

we'll get

```
Hello How are you?
```

Other than that, the two methods are the same.

Let us look at a few examples of how we can use `println()` to display messages to our users. The `print()` method works exactly the same way.

Displaying a simple text message

To display a simple message, we write

```
System.out.println("Hi, my name is Jamie.");
```

Output:

```
Hi, my name is Jamie.
```

Displaying the value of a variable

To display the value of a variable, we pass in the variable name as an argument. For instance, suppose we have

```
int number = 30;
```

we can display the value of `number` by writing

```
System.out.println(number);
```

Output:

```
30
```

Note that we do not enclose the variable name (`number`) in double quotes. If we write

```
System.out.println("number");
```

we'll get

```
number
```

as the output instead.

Displaying results without assigning them to variables

We can also use the `println()` method to display the result of a mathematical expression or a method directly.

For instance, if we write

```
System.out.println(30+5);
```

we'll get

```
35
```

as the output. To display the result of a method, we can write

```
System.out.println("Oracle".substring(1, 4));
```

Here, we are displaying the result of the `substring()` method. We'll get

```
rac
```

as the output.

Using the concatenation sign

Next, let us look at a few examples of how we can display more complex strings by combining two or more shorter strings. To do that, we use the concatenation (+) sign.

For instance, if we write

```
System.out.println("Hello, " + "how are you?" + " I
love Java.");
```

we'll get

```
Hello, how are you? I love Java.
```

To concatenate strings with variables, we can write

```
int results = 79;
System.out.println("You scored " + results + " marks
for your test.");
```

Here, we are concatenating the strings "You scored " and " marks for your test." with the variable `results`. We'll get

```
You scored 79 marks for your test.
```

Finally, we can concatenate strings with mathematical expressions as shown below.

```
System.out.println("The sum of 50 and 2 is " + (50 +
2) + ".");
```

We'll get

```
The sum of 50 and 2 is 52.
```

Note that in the example above, we added parenthesis to the mathematical expression $50+2$. This is to force the compiler to evaluate the expression first before concatenating the result with the other two substrings. You are strongly advised to do so whenever you concatenate strings with mathematical expressions. Failure to do so can result in errors.

5.2 Escape Sequences

Next, let's look at escape sequences. Sometimes in our programs, we may need to print some special "unprintable" characters such as a tab or a newline. In this case, you need to use the \ (backslash) character to escape characters that otherwise have a different meaning.

For instance to print a tab, we type the backslash character before the letter t, like this: \t.

Without the \ character, the letter "t" will be printed. With it, a tab is printed. \t is known as an escape sequence. If you type

```
System.out.println("Hello\tWorld");
```

you'll get

```
Hello     World
```

Other commonly used escape sequences include:

To prints a newline (\n)

Example
```
System.out.println("Hello\nWorld");
```

Output
```
Hello
World
```

To print the backslash character itself (\\)

Example
```
System.out.println("\\");
```

Output
```
\
```

To print double quotes (\") so that the double quote does not end the string

Example
```
System.out.println("I am 5'9\" tall");
```

Output
```
I am 5'9" tall
```

5.3 Formatting Outputs

In the previous examples, we looked at how we can display outputs to users using the `println()` and `print()` methods. However, sometimes we want to have greater control over the format of the output. For instance, if we write

```
System.out.println("The answer for 5.45 divided by 3
is " + (5.45/3));
```

we'll get

```
The answer for 5.45 divided by 3 is
1.8166666666666667
```

In most cases, we do not want to display so many decimal places to our users. In that case, we can use the `printf()` method instead to display the output to our users. The `printf()` method is slightly more complex than the `println()` method, but it offers more control over how our output is displayed. To format the output above, we can write

```
System.out.printf("The answer for %.3f divided by %d
is %.2f.", 5.45, 3, 5.45/3);
```

This will give the output as

```
The answer for 5.450 divided by 3 is 1.82.
```

The `printf()` method requires one or more arguments. In the example above, we passed in four arguments to the method.

The first argument `"The answer for %.3f divided by %d is %.2f."` is the string to be formatted.

You may notice a few weird symbols in the string: `%.3f`, `%d` and `%.2f`. These are known as format specifiers. They serve as placeholders and are replaced by the arguments that follow. The first format specifier (`%.3f`) is replaced by the first argument that follows (`5.45`), the second (`%d`) by the second argument (`3`) and so on.

Format specifiers always begin with a percent sign (`%`) and end with a converter (such as `f` or `d`). They specify how the arguments that replace them should be formatted. In between the percent sign (`%`) and the converter, you can add additional information known as flags.

In our example, the first format specifier is `%.3f`.

`f` is the converter. It tells the compiler that it should be replaced by a floating point number (i.e. numbers with decimal places such as `float` or `double`). If we try to replace it with a non floating point number, we'll get an error.

`.3` is the flag. It indicates that we want to display the number with 3 decimal places. Hence, the number `5.45` is displayed as `5.450` in the output.

Other than the `%.3f` specifier, there are a lot of other specifiers that we can use in Java. The next two sections discuss some of the other commonly used converters and flags in our specifiers.

5.3.1 Converters

The integer converter: d

This converter is for formatting integers such as `byte`, `short`, `int` and `long`.

Example
```
System.out.printf("%d", 12);
```

Output
```
12
```

Note:

`System.out.printf("%d", 12.9);` will give us an error as 12.9 is not an integer.

Similarly, `System.out.printf("%f", 12);` will give us an error as 12 is not a floating point number.

The newline converter: n

This converter moves the cursor to the next line

Example
```
System.out.printf("%d%n%d", 12, 3);
```

Output
```
12
3
```

5.3.2 Flags

The width flag

This flag is used to specify total width.

Example 1
```
System.out.printf("%8d", 12);
```

Output
```
      12
```

In the output above, there are 6 spaces in front of the number 12, giving us a total width of 8.

Example 2
```
System.out.printf("%8.2f", 12.4);
```

Output
```
   12.40
```

In the output above, there are 3 spaces in front of the number, giving us a total width of 8 including the decimal point.

The thousands separator flag (,)

This flag is used to display numbers with a thousands separator

Example 1
```
System.out.printf("%,d", 12345);
```

Output
```
12,345
```

Example 2
```
System.out.printf("%,.2f", 12345.56789);
```

Output
```
12,345.57
```

5.4 Accepting User Input

Now that we know how to display outputs to users, let's look at how we can accept input from them. Accepting input is actually pretty straightforward. There are a few ways to do it, but the easiest and most common way is to use a `Scanner` object.

To accept user input, we need to first import the `Scanner` class using the statement below:

```
import java.util.Scanner;
```

Next, we need to create a `Scanner` object and pass `System.in` as an argument.

`System.in` tells the compiler that you want to get input from the standard input device, which is usually a keyboard. If you are new to programming, you may not understand what an object is. Don't worry about this; you'll learn about classes and objects in Chapter 7. For now, just know that you need to write the statement below to accept inputs from users.

```
Scanner reader = new Scanner(System.in);
```

The `Scanner` class contains a few methods that we can use to read input from the user. The commonly used methods are `nextInt()`, `nextDouble()` and `nextLine()` for reading `int`, `double` and `String` data types respectively.

To understand how these methods work, let's create a new project in NetBeans and name it *InputDemo*. Refer to Chapter 2.2 if you have forgotten how to create a new project in NetBeans. Replace the code with the code below (line numbers are added for reference):

```
1 package inputdemo;
2 import java.util.Scanner;
3
4 public class InputDemo {
5    public static void main(String[] args) {
6       Scanner input = new Scanner(System.in);
7
8       System.out.print("Enter an integer: ");
9       int myInt = input.nextInt();
10      System.out.printf("You entered %d.%n%n",
myInt);
11
12      System.out.print("Enter a double: ");
13      double myDouble = input.nextDouble();
14      System.out.printf("You entered %.2f.%n%n",
myDouble);
15
16      System.out.print("Enter a string: ");
17      input.nextLine();
18      String myString = input.nextLine();
19      System.out.printf("You entered \"%s\".%n%n",
myString);
20
21   }
22}
```

On line 2, we import the `java.util.Scanner` class.

Next, we create a `Scanner` object on line 6 and name it `input`.

On line 8, we prompt the user to enter an integer. We then use the `nextInt()` method to read the integer. Finally on line 10, we display the user's input using the `printf()` method.

From line 12 to 14, we do something similar, except that we prompt the user to enter a `double` and use the `nextDouble()` method to read the input.

From line 16 to 19, we prompt the user to enter a string and use the `nextLine()` method to read the string.

However, you may notice something different here. On line 17, we have an additional statement:

```
input.nextLine();
```

In other words, we called the `nextLine()` method twice (on lines 17 and 18). This is necessary because of how the `nextDouble()` method on line 13 works. The `nextDouble()` method only reads in a `double`. However, whenever the user inputs a number, the user will press the Enter key. This Enter key is essentially the newline character (`"\n"`) and is ignored by the `nextDouble()` method as it is not a `double`. We say that the `nextDouble()` method does not consume the newline character. We need the `nextLine()` method on line 17 to consume this newline character.

If you delete Line 17 and try to run the program again, you'll see that you won't have a chance to key in any string. This is because the `nextLine()` method on line 18 consumes the previous newline character. As there is no other `nextLine()` statement after this, the program will not wait for another input from the user.

Whenever you use the `nextLine()` method after the `nextDouble()` method, you should always have an additional `nextLine()` method to consume the previous newline character. The same applies to the `nextInt()` method. Try running this program and enter an integer, double and string when prompted. The program should run as expected.

Besides the three methods mentioned above, Java also has the `nextByte()`, `nextShort()`, `nextLong()`, `nextFloat()` and `nextBoolean()` methods for reading a `byte`, `short`, `long`, `float` and `boolean` value respectively.

Each of these methods expects to read in values of the correct data type. For instance, the `nextDouble()` method expects to read in a `double`.

If the user does not enter values of the correct data type, the methods will try to convert the input to the correct type. If this fails, the methods result in an error.

For instance, if the `nextDouble()` method reads in the value 20, it'll convert it to a `double`. However, if it reads in the string "hello", it'll generate an error.

We'll learn how to deal with these errors in the next chapter.

Chapter 6: Control Flow Statements

We've covered quite a bit in the previous chapters. By now, you should know the basic structure of a Java program and be able to write a simple Java program that uses variables. In addition, you also learned how you can use the various built-in Java methods to interact with your users.

In this chapter, we are going to take things a step further – we are going to learn how to control the flow of your program. By default, the statements inside your program are executed from top to bottom, in the order that they appear. However, we can alter this flow using control flow statements.

These statements include decision-making statements (`if`, `switch`), looping statements (`for`, `while`, `do-while`), and branching statements (`break`, `continue`). We'll look at each of them in subsequent sections.

For now, let us first look at comparison operators.

6.1 Comparison Operators

Most control flow statements involve doing some form of comparison. The program proceeds differently depending on the result of the comparison.

The most commonly used comparison operator is the equality operator. If we want to compare whether two variables are equal, we use the `==` (double =) operator. For instance, if you write $x == y$, you are asking the program to check if the value of x is equal to the value of y. If they are equal, the condition is met and the statement evaluates to `true`. Else, the statement evaluates to `false`.

In addition to evaluating whether two values are equal, there are other comparison operators that we can use in our control flow statements.

Not equal (!=)

Returns `true` if the left is not equal to the right

5 != 2 is true
6 != 6 is false

Greater than (>)

Returns `true` if the left is greater than the right

5 > 2 is true
3 > 6 is false

Smaller than (<)

Returns `true` if the left is smaller than the right

1 < 7 is true
9 < 6 is false

Greater than or equal to (>=)

Returns `true` if the left is greater than or equal to the right

5 >= 2 is true
5 >= 5 is true
3 >= 6 is false

Smaller than or equal to (<=)

Returns `true` if the left is smaller than or equal to the right

5 <= 7 is true
7 <= 7 is true
9 <= 6 is false

We also have two logical operators (`&&`, `||`) that are useful if we want to combine multiple conditions.

The AND operator (&&)

Returns true if **all** conditions are met

`5==5 && 2>1 && 3!=7` is true
`5==5 && 2<1 && 3!=7` is false as the second condition (`2<1`) is false

The OR operator (||)

Returns true if **at least one** condition is met.

`5==5 || 2<1 || 3==7` is true as the first condition (`5==5`) is true
`5==6 || 2<1 || 3==7` is false as all conditions are false

6.2 Decision Making Statements

Now that we are familiar with comparison operators, let us proceed to learn how we can use these operators to control the flow of a program. We'll look at the `if` statement first.

6.2.1 If Statement

The `if` statement is one of the most commonly used control flow statements. It allows the program to evaluate if a certain condition is met and perform the appropriate action based on the result of the evaluation.

The structure of an `if` statement is as follows (line numbers are added for reference):

```
1   if (condition 1 is met)
2   {
3       do Task A
4   }
```

```
5  else if (condition 2 is met)
6  {
7        do Task B
8  }
9  else if (condition 3 is met)
10 {
11       do Task C
12 }
13 else
14 {
15       do Task D
16 }
```

Line 1 tests the first condition. If the condition is met, everything inside the pair of curly braces that follow (lines 2 to 4) will be executed. The rest of the `if` statement (from line 5 to 16) will be skipped.

If the first condition is not met, you can use the `else if` blocks that follow to test more conditions (lines 5 to 12). There can be multiple `else if` blocks. Finally, you can use the `else` block (lines 13 to 16) to execute some code if none of the preceding conditions are met. The `else if` and `else` blocks are optional. You do not need to include them if there are no additional conditions to test.

To fully understand how the `if` statement works, let's try an example. Launch NetBeans and create a new project called *IfDemo*. Replace the code generated with the following code.

```
package ifdemo;
import java.util.Scanner;

public class IfDemo{

    public static void main(String[] arg)
    {

        Scanner input = new Scanner(System.in);
```

```java
System.out.print("\nPlease enter your age: ");
int userAge = input.nextInt();
if (userAge < 0 || userAge > 100)
{
    System.out.println("Invalid Age");
    System.out.println("Age must be between 0
and 100");
}
else if (userAge < 18)
    System.out.println("Sorry you are
underage");
else if (userAge < 21)
    System.out.println("You need parental
consent");
else
{
    System.out.println("Congratulations!");
    System.out.println("You may sign up for the
event!");
}
}
}
```

The program first prompts the user for his age and stores the result in the userAge variable. The statement

```java
if (userAge < 0 || userAge > 100)
```

checks if the value of userAge is smaller than zero or greater than 100. If either of the conditions is true, the program will execute all statements within the curly braces that follow. In this example, it'll print "Invalid Age", followed by "Age must be between 0 and 100".

On the other hand, if both conditions are false, the program will test the next condition - else if (userAge < 18). If userAge is less than 18 (but more than or equal to 0 since the first condition is not met), the program will print "Sorry you are underage".

You may notice that we did not enclose the statement

```
System.out.println("Sorry you are underage");
```

in curly braces. This is because curly braces are optional if there is only one statement to execute.

If the user did not enter a value smaller than 18, but entered a value greater than or equal to 18 but smaller than 21, the next else if statement will be executed. In this case, the message "You need parental consent" will be printed.

Finally, if the user entered a value greater than or equal to 21 but smaller than or equal to 100, the program will execute the code in the else block. In this case, it will print "Congratulations" followed by "You may sign up for the event!".

Run the program five times and enter -1, 8, 20, 23 and 121 respectively for each run. You'll get the following outputs:

```
Please enter your age: -1
Invalid Age
Age must be between 0 and 100

Please enter your age: 8
Sorry you are underage

Please enter your age: 20
You need parental consent

Please enter your age: 23
Congratulations!
You may sign up for the event!

Please enter your age: 121
Invalid Age
```

```
Age must be between 0 and 100
```

6.2.2 Ternary Operator

The ternary operator (?) is a simpler form of an `if` statement that is very convenient if you want to assign a value to a variable depending on the result of a condition. The syntax is:

```
condition ? value to return if condition is true :
value to return if condition is false;
```

For instance, the statement

```
3>2 ? 10 : 5;
```

returns the value 10 since 3 is greater than 2 (i.e. the condition `3 > 2` is true). This value can then be assigned to a variable.

If we write

```
int myNum = 3>2 ? 10 : 5;
```

`myNum` will be assigned the value 10.

6.2.3 Switch Statement

The `switch` statement is similar to an `if` statement except that it does not work with a range of values. A `switch` statement requires each case to be based on a single value. Depending on the value of the variable used for switching, the program will execute the correct block of code.

The syntax of a switch statement is as follows:

```
switch (variable used for switching)
{
    case firstCase:
```

```
        do A;
        break;

    case secondCase:
        do B;
        break;

    default:
        do C;
        break;
}
```

You can have as many cases as you want when using a `switch` statement. The `default` case is optional and is executed if no other case applies. You can use either a `byte`, `short`, `char` or `int` variable for switching. Starting from Java 7, you can also use a `String` variable for switching.

When a certain case is satisfied, everything starting from the next line is executed until a `break` statement is reached. A `break` statement instructs the program to break out of the `switch` statement and continue executing the rest of the program.

Let's look at an example of how the `switch` statement works. To try this example, launch NetBeans and create a new project called *SwitchDemo*. Replace the code generated with the following code. In this example, we use a `String` variable for switching.

```
1   package switchdemo;
2   import java.util.Scanner;
3
4   public class SwitchDemo{
5
6     public static void main(String[] args) {
7
8         Scanner input = new Scanner(System.in);
9
```

```
10      System.out.print("Enter your grade: ");
11      String userGrade =
input.nextLine().toUpperCase();
12
13      switch (userGrade)
14      {
15          case "A+":
16          case "A":
17              System.out.println("Distinction");
18              break;
19          case "B":
20              System.out.println("B Grade");
21              break;
22          case "C":
23              System.out.println("C Grade");
24              break;
25          default:
26              System.out.println("Fail");
27              break;
28      }
29  }
30 }
```

The program first prompts the user for his grade on line 10. Next, on line 11, it reads in the user's input and stores the result in userGrade using the statement below:

```
String userGrade = input.nextLine().toUpperCase();
```

This statement may look a bit unfamiliar to some readers. Here, we are calling two methods in the same statement.

```
input.nextLine()
```

first reads the input that the user entered. This method returns a string. We then use the resulting string to call the toUpperCase() method. This statement shows an example of how you can call two methods in the same statement. The methods are executed from left to right. That is, the `nextLine()` method is executed first followed by the `toUpperCase()` method.

We have to convert user input to upper case before assigning it to `userGrade` because Java is case-sensitive. We want the program to display "Distinction" regardless of whether the user entered "A" or "a". Hence, we convert any lower case input to upper case first before assigning it to `userGrade`.

After getting the user's grade, we use the `switch` statement that follows to determine the output.

If the grade entered is "A+" (Line 15), the program executes the next statement until it reaches the `break` statement. This means it'll execute Line 16 to 18. Thus the output is "Distinction".

If grade is "A" (Line 16), the program executes Line 17 and 18. Similarly, the output is "Distinction".

If grade is not "A+" or "A", the program checks the next case. It keeps checking from top to bottom until a case is satisfied. If none of the cases applies, the `default` case is executed.

If you run the code above, you'll get the following output for each of the input shown:

```
Enter your grade: A+
Distinction

Enter your grade: A
Distinction

Enter your grade: B
B Grade

Enter your grade: C
```

```
C Grade

Enter your grade: D
Fail

Enter your grade: Hello
Fail
```

6.3 Looping Statements

Now, let us look at looping statements in Java. The four commonly used looping statements in Java are the `for` statement, the enhanced `for` statement, the `while` statement and the `do-while` statement.

6.3.1 For Statement

The `for` statement executes a block of code repeatedly until the test condition is no longer valid.

The syntax for a `for` statement is as follows:

```
for (initial value; test condition; modification to
value)
{
    //Do Some Task
}
```

To understand how the `for` statement works, let's consider the example below.

```
1 for (int i = 0; i < 5; i++)
2 {
3     System.out.println(i);
4 }
```

The main focus of the `for` statement is Line 1:

```
for (int i = 0; i < 5; i++)
```

There are three parts to it, each separated by a semi-colon.

The first part declares and initializes an `int` variable `i` to zero. This variable serves as a loop counter.

The second part tests if `i` is smaller than 5. If it is, the statements inside the curly braces will be executed. In this example, the curly braces are optional as there is only one statement.

After executing the `System.out.println(i)` statement, the program returns to the last segment in Line 1. `i++` increments the value of `i` by 1. Hence, `i` is increased from 0 to 1.

After the increment, the program tests if the new value of `i` is still smaller than 5. If it is, it executes the `System.out.println(i)` statement once again.

This process of testing and incrementing the loop counter is repeated until the condition `i < 5` is no longer `true`. At this point, the program exits the `for` statement and continues to execute other commands after the statement.

The output for the code segment is:

```
0
1
2
3
4
```

The output stops at 4 because when `i` is 5, the `System.out.println(i)` statement is not executed as 5 is not smaller than 5.

The `for` statement is commonly used to loop through an array. For instance, if we have

```
int[] myNumbers = {10, 20, 30, 40, 50};
```

we can use a `for` statement and the `length` field of the array to loop through the array as shown below.

```
for (int i = 0; i < myNumbers.length; i++)
{
    System.out.println(myNumbers[i]);
}
```

As `myNumbers.length` is equal to 5, this code runs from `i = 0` to `i = 4`. If we run the code, we'll get the following output:

```
10
20
30
40
50
```

6.3.2 Enhanced For Statement

In addition to the `for` statement, we can also use an enhanced `for` statement when working with arrays and Collections (we'll talk about Collections in Chapter 9). An enhanced `for` statement is very useful if you want to get information from an array without making any changes to it.

The syntax for an enhanced `for` statement is:

```
for (variable declaration : name of array)
{

}
```

Suppose you have

```
int[] myNumbers = {10, 20, 30, 40, 50};
```

You can use the following code to display the elements of the array.

```
for (int item : myNumbers)
    System.out.println(item);
```

In the code above, we declared an int variable item that is used for looping. Each time the loop runs, an element in the myNumbers array is assigned to the variable item. For instance, the first time the loop runs, the integer 10 is assigned to item.

The line

```
System.out.println(item);
```

then prints out the number 10.

The second time the loop runs, the integer 20 is assigned to item. The line

```
System.out.println(item);
```

prints out the number 20.

This continues until all the elements in the array have been printed.

6.3.3 While Statement

Next, let us look at the while statement. Like the name suggests, a while statement repeatedly executes instructions inside the loop while a certain condition remains valid. The structure of a while statement is as follows:

```
while (condition is true)
{
    do A
}
```

Most of the time when using a `while` statement, we need to first declare a variable to function as a loop counter. Let's call this variable `counter`. The code below shows an example of how a `while` statement works.

```
int counter = 5;

while (counter > 0)
{
    System.out.println("Counter = " + counter);
    counter = counter - 1;
}
```

If you run the code, you'll get the following output

```
Counter = 5
Counter = 4
Counter = 3
Counter = 2
Counter = 1
```

A `while` statement has a relatively simple syntax. The statements inside the curly braces are executed as long as `counter > 0`.

Notice that we have the line `counter = counter - 1` inside the curly braces? This line is crucial. It decreases the value of `counter` by 1 each time the loop is run.

We need to decrease the value of `counter` by 1 so that the loop condition (`counter > 0`) will eventually evaluate to `false`. If we forget to do that, the loop will keep running endlessly, resulting in an infinite loop. The program will keep printing `counter = 5` until you somehow kill the program. Not a pleasant experience especially if you have a large program and you have no idea which code segment is causing the infinite loop.

6.3.4 Do-while Statement

The do-while statement is similar to the while statement with one main difference - the code within the curly braces of a do-while statement is executed at least once. Here's an example of how a do-while statement works.

```
int counter = 100;

do {
    System.out.println("Counter = " + counter);
    counter++;
} while (counter<0);
```

As the test condition (while (counter<0)) is placed after the closing curly brace, it is tested after the code inside the curly braces is executed at least once.

If you run the code above, you will get

```
Counter = 100;
```

After the System.out.println("Counter = " + counter); statement is executed for the first time, counter is incremented by 1. The value of counter is now 101. When the program reaches the test condition, the test fails as counter is not smaller than 0. The program will then exit the loop. Even though the original value of counter does not meet the test condition (counter < 0), the code inside the curly braces is still executed once.

Note that for a do-while statement, a semi-colon (;) is required after the test condition.

6.4 Branching Statements

We've now covered most of the control flow statements in Java. Next, let us look at branching statements.

A branching statement is a statement that instructs the program to branch to another line of code. Branching statements are commonly used in loops and other control flow statements.

6.4.1 Break Statement

The first branching statement is the break statement. We have already seen how this statement can be used in a switch statement. In addition to using it in a switch statement, the break statement can also be used in other control flow statements. It causes the program to exit a loop prematurely when a certain condition is met. Let us look at an example of how the break statement can be used in a for statement.

Consider the code segment below:

```
1 for (int i = 0; i < 5; i++)
2 {
3    System.out.println("i = " + i);
4    if (i == 2)
5        break;
6 }
```

In this example, we used an if statement inside a for statement. It is very common for us to 'mix-and-match' various control flow statements in programming, such as using a while statement inside an if statement or using a for statement inside a while statement. This is known as a nested control statement.

If you run the code segment above, you will get the following output.

```
i =  0
i =  1
```

```
i =  2
```

Notice that the loop ends prematurely at i = 2?

Without the break statement, the loop should run from i = 0 to i = 4 because the loop condition is i < 5. However with the break statement, when i = 2, the condition on line 4 evaluates to true. The break statement on line 5 then causes the loop to end prematurely.

6.4.2 Continue Statement

Another commonly used branching statement is the continue statement. When we use continue, the rest of the loop after the word is skipped for that iteration. An example will make it clearer.

If you run the code segment below

```
1 for (int i = 0; i<5; i++)
2 {
3    System.out.println("i = " + i);
4    if (i == 2)
5       continue;
6    System.out.println("I will not be printed if i=2.");
7 }
```

You will get the following output:

```
i =  0
I will not be printed if i=2.
i =  1
I will not be printed if i=2.
i =  2
i =  3
I will not be printed if i=2.
i =  4
```

```
I will not be printed if i=2.
```

When $i = 2$, the line after the continue statement is not executed. The program jumps back to line 1 and continues executing from there. Everything runs as per normal after that.

6.5 Exception Handling

We now know how to control the flow of a program under 'normal' circumstances using control flow statements. Let us now learn how to control the flow of a program when an error occurs. This is known as exception handling.

When we code a program, we should always try to pre-empt possible errors. If we believe that a certain block of code may cause an error, we should try to manage it using the `try-catch-finally` statement. The syntax for the `try-catch-finally` statement is as follows:

```
try
{
    do something
}
catch (type of error)
{
    do something else when an error occurs
}
finally
{
    do this regardless of whether the try or catch
condition is met.
}
```

You can have more than one `catch` blocks. In addition, the `finally` block is optional.

Let's consider an example. Launch NetBeans and create a new project called *ErrorDemo*. Replace the generated code with the following:

```
1 package errordemo;
2 import java.util.Scanner;
3
4 public class ErrorDemo{
5    public static void main(String[] args) {
6
7        int num, deno;
8
9        Scanner input = new Scanner(System.in);
10
11       try
12       {
13           System.out.print("Please enter the
numerator: ");
14           num = input.nextInt();
15
16           System.out.print("Please enter the
denominator: ");
17           deno = input.nextInt();
18
19           System.out.println("The result is " +
num/deno);
20
21       }
22       catch (Exception e)
23       {
24           System.out.println(e.getMessage());
25       }
26       finally
27       {
28           System.out.println("---- End of Error
Handling Example ----");
29       }
30   }
```

```
31 }
```

In this example, the `try` block is from line 11 to 21, the `catch` block is from line 22 to 25 and the `finally` block is from line 26 to 29.

If you run the code and enter 12 and 4, you'll get the message

```
The result is 3
---- End of Error Handling Example ----
```

In this case, the program tries to execute the code in the `try` block and does it successfully. Hence, it displays the result of the division. After the code in the `try` block is executed, the code in the `finally` block is executed. The `finally` block is always executed regardless of whether the `try` or `catch` block is executed.

Now, run the program again and enter 12 and 0 instead. You'll get

```
/ by zero
---- End of Error Handling Example ----
```

In this case, the program tries to execute the code in the `try` block and fails. This is because you cannot divide a number by zero. Hence, the code in the `catch` block is executed instead. After the `catch` block is executed, the code in the `finally` block is executed as well.

The `catch` block allows us to specify the type of error that it should catch. In our example, we are trying to catch a general error. Therefore, we write

```
catch (Exception e)
```

where `Exception` refers to the class that the error belongs to and `e` is the name given to the error.

`Exception` is a pre-written class in Java. It handles all general errors and has a method called `getMessage()` that explains the reason for the exception. To display the error message, we write

```
System.out.println(e.getMessage());
```

In our example, we get the following error message

```
/ by zero
```

6.5.1 Specific Errors

In the example above, we used the `Exception` class to catch a general error. In addition to the `Exception` class, Java has other classes that can handle more specific errors. This is useful if you want to perform specific tasks depending on the error caught. For instance, you may want to display your own error messages.

To see how this works, launch NetBeans and create a new project called *ErrorDemo2*. Replace the code with the following code:

```
package errordemo2;

import java.util.InputMismatchException;
import java.util.Scanner;

public class ErrorDemo2{

    public static void main(String[] args) {

        int choice = 0;

        Scanner input = new Scanner(System.in);

        int[] numbers = { 10, 11, 12, 13, 14, 15 };
        System.out.print("Please enter the index of the
array: ");
```

```
    try
    {
        choice = input.nextInt();
        System.out.printf("numbers[%d] = %d%n",
choice, numbers[choice]);
    }catch (ArrayIndexOutOfBoundsException e)
    {
        System.out.println("Error: Index is
invalid.");
    }catch (InputMismatchException e)
    {
        System.out.println("Error: You did not enter
an integer.");
    }catch (Exception e)
    {
        System.out.printf(e.getMessage());
    }
}
}
```

If you enter

```
10
```

You will get

```
Error: Index is invalid.
```

If you enter

```
Hello
```

You will get

```
Error: You did not enter an integer.
```

The first error is an `ArrayIndexOutOfBoundsException` exception and was handled by the first `catch` block. This exception occurs when you try to access an element of an array with an index that is outside its bounds.

The second error is an `InputMismatchException` exception and was handled by the second `catch` block. The `InputMismatchException` exception occurs when the input received by a `Scanner` method does not match the expected type. In our example, `input.nextInt()` generated an `InputMismatchException` error because the input "Hello" is not an integer, which is the data type expected by the `nextInt()` method.

After the two specific `catch` blocks, we have one more `catch` block to catch any general errors that we did not pre-empt.

The example above shows three of the many exceptions in Java.

The `InputMismatchExpection` class is found in the `java.util` `package` and must be imported before it can be used. In contrast, the other two exception classes (`ArrayIndexOutOfBoundsException` and `Exception`) are found in `java.lang` and are imported by default is all Java programs. Do not worry if you cannot remember which exception classes need to be imported and which are imported by default; NetBeans will prompt you whenever you need to import any package or class yourself.

6.5.2 Throwing Exceptions

Next, let us look at how to throw exceptions. In the example above, we try to catch errors under pre-defined conditions.

For instance, we catch the `ArrayIndexOutOfBoundsException` error when users try to access an element of an array with an index that is outside its bounds. In the example above, that will be when users enter a negative number or a positive number greater than 5.

In addition to catching errors under pre-defined conditions, we can also define our own conditions for when an error should occur. This is known as throwing an exception.

Suppose for whatever reason, you do not want users to access the first element of the array. You can do that by forcing an exception to be triggered when users enter the number 0.

To understand how this works, try running the previous program and enter the value 0. You'll notice that the program runs normally and gives you

```
numbers[0] = 10
```

as the output.

Now try adding the statements

```
if (choice == 0)
    throw new ArrayIndexOutOfBoundsException();
```

after the statement

```
choice = input.nextInt();
```

in the try block above. Run the program again and enter the value 0. You'll notice that the

```
catch(ArrayIndexOutOfBoundsException e)
```

block is executed instead.

This is because when users enter the value 0, the condition choice == 0 evaluates to true. Hence, the statement

```
throw new ArrayIndexOutOfBoundsException();
```

is executed. This statement causes the

`catch(ArrayIndexOutOfBoundsException e)`

block to be executed.

Chapter 7: Object Oriented Programming Part 1

In this chapter, we are going to look at a very important concept in Java programming – the concept of object-oriented programming.

We'll learn what object-oriented programming is and how to write our own classes and create objects from them. In addition, we'll also discuss the concept of fields, getters and setters, constructors and methods.

7.1 What is Object-Oriented Programming?

Simply stated, object-oriented programming is an approach to programming that breaks a programming problem into objects that interact with each other.

Objects are created from templates known as classes. You can think of a class as the blueprint of a building. An object is the actual "building" that we build based on the blueprint.

7.2 Writing our own class

The syntax for declaring a class is as follows:

```
AccessModifier class ClassName {
    //Contents of the class
    //including fields, constructors and methods
}
```

An example is

```
public class ManagementStaff{

}
```

In the example above, we first state the access level of the class using an access modifier. Access modifiers are like gate keepers, they control who has access to that class. In other words, they control whether other classes can use a particular field or method in that class.

A class can either be `public` or package-private. In the example above, the class is `public`.

`public` means the class can be accessed by any class in the program.

Package-private, on the other hand, means the class is only accessible to other classes within the same package. There can be more than one packages within a single Java application. Refer to Chapter 2.3.1 if you have forgotten what a package is. Package-private is the default access level. If we do not write any access modifier, it means the class is package-private.

We'll look at access modifiers in greater depth in Chapter 8.5.

After declaring the access level of the class, we type the `class` keyword to indicate that we are declaring a class, followed by the name of the class (`ManagementStaff`).

It is common practice to use PascalCasing when naming our classes. PascalCasing refers to the practice of capitalizing the first letter of each word, including the first word (e.g. `ThisIsAClassName`). This is the convention that we'll be following in the book.

The contents of the class are enclosed within the pair of curly braces that follows the class name. Contents of a class include constructors, fields, methods, interfaces, and other classes. We'll cover some of them in this chapter.

Now, let's build a class from scratch together.

First, launch NetBeans and create a new Java Application called *ObjectOrientedDemo*.

Study the code that is generated for you. Notice that NetBeans has automatically created a public class for you?

This public class is called `ObjectOrientedDemo` and has the same name as the file, which is called *ObjectOrientedDemo.java*. In Java, there can only be one public class per java file and that public class must have the same name as the file. The `main()` method is inside this public class.

For this example, we are going to create a **second** Java class that interacts with the `ObjectOrientedDemo` class. We'll create this class inside the `objectorienteddemo` package. To do that, right-click on the package name in Project Explorer and select **New > Java Class**. It is important that you click on the correct item in Project Explorer when creating a new class. For instance, if you are adding a new class to the `objectorienteddemo` package, make sure you click on the package name when creating the class (refer to image below).

Right click on the package name

We'll call this new class `Staff` and add fields, constructors and methods to the class. The declaration of the class is as follows:

```
public class Staff {
    //Contents of the class
}
```

We'll be adding fields, methods and constructors to this class. It is important that you type the contents of the class inside the opening and closing braces of the class. If you type them in the wrong location, the program will not run. The complete code for this chapter can be downloaded at http://www.learncodingfast.com/java.

7.2.1 Fields

We'll first declare the fields for our `Staff` class. To do that, add the following lines of code <u>inside the curly braces of the class</u>.

```
private String nameOfStaff;
private final int hourlyRate = 30;
private int hoursWorked;
```

Here, we declare one `String` variable (`nameOfStaff`) and two `int` variables (`hourlyRate` and `hoursWorked`). These variables are known as fields of the class. A field is simply a variable that is declared inside a class. Like any other variables, they are used to store data.

All the three fields are declared as `private`.

We can declare a field as either `private`, `public` or `protected`. If we choose not to state the access level of a class member, it is taken to be package-private by default (i.e. only accessible to other classes within the same package). In our case, we declared the three fields as `private`. This means they can only be accessed from within the `Staff` class itself. Other classes, such as the `ObjectOrientedDemo` class, cannot access these fields.

There are two reasons why we do not want other classes to access these fields.

The first reason is that there is no need for other classes to know about these fields. For instance, in our case, the field `hourlyRate` is only needed within the `Staff` class. We have a method inside the `Staff` class that uses `hourlyRate` to calculate the monthly salary of an employee. Other classes do not use the `hourlyRate` field at all. Hence, it is appropriate to declare `hourlyRate` as `private` so as to hide this field from other classes.

This is known as encapsulation. Encapsulation enables a class to hide data and behaviour from other classes that do not need to know about them. This makes it easier for us to make changes to our code in future if necessary. We can safely change the value of `hourlyRate` without affecting other classes.

The second reason for declaring a field as `private` is that we do not want other classes to freely modify them. This helps to prevent the fields from being corrupted.

We'll talk more about access modifiers in the next chapter.

In addition to the `private` keyword, we also added the `final` keyword when we declared the `hourlyRate` field.

```
private final int hourlyRate = 30;
```

The `final` keyword indicates that the value cannot be changed after it is created. Any variable that is declared as `final` must be initialized at the point of declaration or within the constructor (we'll talk about constructors later). In our example, we initialized `hourlyRate` to 30 when declaring it. This value cannot be changed subsequently anywhere in the code.

7.2.2 Methods

Next, let us look at methods.

A method is a code block that performs a certain task.

Let's add a simple method to our `Staff` class. Remember, you have to add this method inside the opening and closing braces of the `Staff` class.

```
public void printMessage ()
{
    System.out.println("Calculating Pay…");
}
```

This method is declared as

```
public void printMessage ()
{
}
```

The method declaration first states the access level of the method. Here we declared the method as `public` so that the method is accessible everywhere in the program (not just within the `Staff` class).

Next, we state the return type of the method. A method may return a certain result after performing its task. If the method does not return any result, we use the `void` keyword like in our example.

Finally, we state the name of the method (`printMessage` in our example).

The parenthesis () after the method name is where we include the parameters of the method. Parameters are names given to data that we pass in to the method in order for it to perform its task. If the method requires no data (like in our example), we just add a pair of empty parenthesis after the method name.

After we declare the method, we define what it does inside the pair of curly braces that follow. This is known as implementing the method. In our example, the `printMessage ()` method simply prints the line "Calculating Pay…".

That's all there is to the `printMessage ()` method.

Let's move on to a more complex method. This second method

calculates the pay of each employee and returns the result of the calculation. Add the following lines of code to `Staff`.

```
public int calculatePay()
{
    printMessage();

    int staffPay;
    staffPay = hoursWorked * hourlyRate ;

    if (hoursWorked > 0)
       return staffPay;
    else
       return -1;
}
```

This method is declared as

```
public int calculatePay()
{
}
```

The `int` keyword indicates that this method returns a value that is of `int` type.

Inside the curly braces, we have the statement

```
printMessage();
```

This is known as calling or invoking the `printMessage()` method. When the program reaches this statement, it will execute the `printMessage()` method that we wrote earlier and print the line "Calculating Pay..." first before executing the rest of the `calculatePay()` method. This example demonstrates how you can call one method inside another method.

Next, we declare a local variable called `staffPay` and assign the product of the private fields `hourlyRate` and `hoursWorked` to it.

A method can access all the fields that are declared inside the class. In addition, it can declare its own variables. These are known as local variables and only exist within the method. An example is the `staffPay` variable in our example.

After assigning the `staffPay` variable, the `calculatePay()` method uses an `if` statement to determine what result the method should return.

A method usually has at least one return statement. `return` is a keyword that is used to return an answer from the method. There can be more than one return statement in a method. However, once the method executes a return statement, the method will exit.

In our example, if `hoursWorked` is greater than zero, the program will execute the statement

```
return staffPay;
```

and exit the method. This return value can then be assigned to a variable. We'll see how to do that in our `main()` method later.

On the other hand, if `hoursWorked` is less than or equal to zero, the program will execute the statement

```
return -1;
```

and exit the method.

There may be cases where a method does not need to return an answer but simply uses the return statement to exit the method. We'll look at an example of this when we work through our project at the end of the book.

Overloading

Next, let's look at overloading. In Java (and most other languages), you can create two methods of the same name as long as they have different signatures. This is known as overloading. The signature of a method refers to the name of the method and the parameters that it has.

Add the following method below the previous `calculatePay()` method.

```
public int calculatePay(int bonus, int allowance)
{
    printMessage();
    if (hoursWorked > 0)
        return hoursWorked * hourlyRate + bonus +
allowance;
    else
        return 0;
}
```

The signature of the first method is `calculatePay()` while that of the second method is `calculatePay(int bonus, int allowance)`.

This second method has two parameters - `bonus` and `allowance`. It calculates the pay of the employees by adding the values of these two parameters to the product of `hoursWorked` and `hourlyRate`. In this example, we did not use a local variable to store the result of `hoursWorked * hourlyRate + bonus + allowance`. We simply return the result of the computation directly. This is perfectly fine. We'll learn how to use this method later.

Getter and Setter Methods

Now, let us write the getter and setter methods for the class. We'll do that for the `hoursWorked` field.

Recall that the `hoursWorked` field is declared as `private`? This means that the field is not accessible anywhere outside the `Staff` class. However, there may be cases where the field is needed by other classes. In cases like these, we have to write setter and getter methods to allow other classes to access these private fields.

This may sound like a contradiction. Earlier, we mentioned that we use private fields so that other classes do not have access to them. If that is the case, why are we allowing access to them via getter and setter methods?

One of the main reasons is that using getter and setter methods gives us greater control over what rights other classes have when assessing these private fields. We'll see how to do that now.

Add the following setter method to the `Staff` class.

```
public void setHoursWorked(int hours)
{
    if (hours>0)
       hoursWorked = hours;
    else
    {
       System.out.println("Error: HoursWorked Cannot
be Smaller than Zero");
       System.out.println("Error: HoursWorked is not
updated");
    }
}
```

It is a convention for us to name setter methods with the word 'set' followed by the name of the field.

In the setter method above, we accept a parameter called hours and use that to set the value of the `hoursWorked` field. However, we did a simple check first. If the value of hours is more than zero, we assign it to hoursWorked. Else, we do not assign it to hoursWorked and print an error message instead.

This example demonstrates how we can use a setter method to control what values can be assigned to our private field.

In addition to setter methods, we can also write a getter method for our private field. Add the following code to your Staff class. It is a convention for us to name getter methods with the word 'get' followed by the name of the field.

```
public int getHoursWorked()
{
    return hoursWorked;
}
```

This method simply returns the value of the hoursWorked field.

7.2.3 Constructors

Now, let us look at constructors.

A constructor is a block of code (similar to a method) that is used to 'construct' an object from the class template. It always has the same name as the class (Staff in our case) and is commonly used to initialize the fields of the class.

The main feature of a constructor is that it is the first block of code that is called whenever we create an object from our class. Other than that, a constructor is pretty much like a method. However, a constructor does not return any value and we do not have to use the void keyword when declaring a constructor.

Let's learn how to declare a constructor for our Staff class.

Add the following lines to the Staff class.

```
public Staff(String name)
{
    nameOfStaff = name;
    System.out.println("\n" + nameOfStaff);
    System.out.println("--------------------------
");
}
```

In the example above, the constructor accepts a parameter called name and uses it to initialize the nameOfStaff field. It then displays the value of nameOfStaff on the screen and underlines it with a series of dashes. That's all that it does. We'll learn how to use this constructor to 'construct' our objects later.

Next, let's add another constructor to our class. Similar to methods, we can have more than one constructor as long as the signature is different.

```
public Staff(String firstName, String lastName)
{
    nameOfStaff = firstName + " " + lastName;
    System.out.println("\n" + nameOfStaff);
    System.out.println ("--------------------------
");
}
```

This second constructor has two parameters - firstName and lastName. The first line concatenates the two strings and assigns the resulting string to nameOfStaff. The next two lines print nameOfStaff on the screen and underline it with a series of dashes.

Declaring a constructor is optional. If we do not declare our own constructor, NetBeans will automatically generate a default constructor for us. This default constructor does not have any parameter. It initializes any uninitialized fields to their default values, which is 0 or its equivalent, depending on the data type. For instance, the default value for numerical data type is 0 while that for a reference data type is null (which simply means the variable does not store any address).

7.3 Instantiating an Object

Now that we have coded our `Staff` class, let's look at how we can make use of the class to create an object. This process is known as instantiating an object. An object is also known as an instance.

To recap, our `Staff` class has the following components:

Fields

```
private String nameOfStaff;
private final int hourlyRate = 30;
private int hoursWorked;
```

Methods

```
public void printMessage()
public int calculatePay()
public int calculatePay(int bonus, int allowance)
public void setHoursWorked(int hours)
public int getHoursWorked()
```

Constructors

```
public Staff(String name)
public Staff(String firstName, String lastName)
```

We shall instantiate a `Staff` object in the `main()` method inside our `ObjectOrientedDemo` class.

The syntax for instantiating an object is

```
ClassName objectName = new ClassName(arguments);
```

To do that, double click on the filename *ObjectOrientedDemo.java* in the Projects window and add the following lines inside the curly braces of the `main()` method.

```
Staff staff1 = new Staff("Peter");
staff1.setHoursWorked(160);
int pay = staff1.calculatePay(1000, 400);
System.out.println("Pay = " + pay);
```

The first statement

```
Staff staff1 = new Staff("Peter");
```

uses the first constructor (with one parameter) to instantiate our `staff1` object.

Once we create the `staff1` object, we can use the dot operator after the object's name to access any public field or method in the Staff class. We have to use the dot operator here because we are trying to access members of the `Staff` class from within the `ObjectOrientedDemo` class. The dot operator is necessary whenever we want to access a field or method from another class.

If you are accessing members of the same class, you do not need to use the dot operator. An example is when we called the `printMessage()` method from the `calculatePay()` method earlier. We did not use the dot operator as both methods are from the same class.

After creating our `staff1` object, the next line shows how we can use the public setter method `setHoursWorked()` to assign a value to the `hoursWorked` field.

```
staff1.setHoursWorked(160);
```

Here, we set the `hoursWorked` field to 160. If we try to access the `hoursWorked` field directly by writing

```
staff1.hoursWorked = 160;
```

we will get an error as `hoursWorked` is a private field and is therefore only accessible within the `Staff` class.

Next, we call the `calculatePay()` method by writing

```
staff1.calculatePay(1000, 400);
```

In this example, as we have the numbers 1000 and 400 inside the parenthesis, we are using the second `calculatePay()` method. We are passing in the values 1000 and 400 to the parameters `bonus` and `allowance` respectively. The values that we passed in are known as arguments. The program then uses that method to calculate the pay and return the answer. This answer is assigned to the variable `pay`.

Finally, we use the `System.out.println()` method to display the value of `pay` on the screen.

If you run the code above, you will get

```
Peter
-------------------------
Calculating Pay...
Pay = 6200
```

Play around with the code a bit to get a better feel of how classes work. Try adding the following lines of code

```
Staff staff2 = new Staff("Jane", "Lee");
staff2.setHoursWorked(160);
pay = staff2.calculatePay();
System.out.println("Pay = " + pay);
```

Here, we used the second constructor (with 2 parameters) to instantiate `staff2`. If you run the code above, you will get

```
Jane Lee
-------------------------
Calculating Pay...
Pay = 4800
```

Now, let us add some code to demonstrate how data validation works when we use setter methods. Add the following lines of code to your `main()` method.

```
System.out.println("\n\nUpdating Jane's Hours Worked
to -10");
staff2.setHoursWorked(-10);
System.out.println("\nHours Worked =  " +
staff2.getHoursWorked());
pay = staff2.calculatePay();
System.out.println("Pay = " + pay);
```

Here, we try to set the value of `hoursWorked` to -10. If you run the code above, you'll get

```
Updating Jane's Hours Worked to -10
Error: HoursWorked Cannot be Smaller than Zero
Error: HoursWorked is not updated

Hours Worked = 160
Calculating Pay...
Pay = 4800
```

As -10 is not a valid value for `hoursWorked`, the setter method does not update the field for Jane (`staff2`). Hence, when we use the getter method to get the value of `hoursWorked`, we realise that it remains as 160.

The example above shows how we can use setter methods to control what values our fields can take. We should always do these data validations inside the class that contains the private field itself. If we do not do that, we will have to rely on whoever is using the `Staff` class to do the validation which is risky.

7.4 Static

We've covered some pretty complicated concepts in this chapter. You now know what a class is, including what fields, methods and constructors are. You also learned how to declare and use a class. If you are new to object oriented programming, I strongly suggest that you download the complete program for this chapter from http://www.learncodingfast.com/java and play around with it. Study the code and make sure you fully understand the topics covered in this chapter so far before moving on.

In this section, we'll look at another keyword that is used in object oriented programming – the keyword `static`.

Previously, we looked at how we can use the `Staff` class to create our `staff1` and `staff2` objects. We then used these objects to call the methods inside the `Staff` class (e.g. `staff1.calculatePay(1000, 400)`).

Now suppose we want to call some methods or access some fields in the `Staff` class <u>without creating a `Staff` object</u>. Would that be possible?

The answer is yes. We have to use the `static` keyword.

To understand the `static` keyword, consider the code below. Launch NetBeans and create a new Java application called *StaticDemo*. Replace the code with the code below:

```
package staticdemo;

class MyClass
{
    //Non static field and method
    public String message = "Hello World";
    public void displayMessage()
    {
        System.out.println("Message = " + message);
```

```
        }

    //Static field and method
    public static String greetings = "Good morning";
    public static void displayGreetings()
    {
        System.out.println("Greeting = " + greetings);
    }
}

public class StaticDemo {
    public static void main(String[] args) {

        MyClass sd = new MyClass();

        System.out.println(sd.message);
        sd.displayMessage();

        System.out.println(MyClass.greetings);
        MyClass.displayGreetings();
    }
}
```

In the example above, we created two classes called MyClass and StaticDemo.

In this example, we created them within one file. If you prefer, you can separate the two classes into separate files. It is considered good practice to separate classes into separate files whenever possible. However for simplicity, we'll use a single file in this example. In addition, we declared the fields as public to shorten the code. In practice, you are strongly encouraged to make your fields private and use getter and setter methods instead.

In our example, MyClass contains one non static field message and one non static method displayMessage().

It also contains one static field `greetings` and one static method `displayGreetings()`.

To access the <u>non static</u> members of `MyClass` from another class, we need to instantiate an object as before. We did that inside the `main()` method of the `StaticDemo` class.

```
MyClass sd = new MyClass();

System.out.println(sd.message);
sd.displayMessage();
```

However, to access the <u>static</u> members, we do not need to create any object. We simply use the class name to access them as shown below.

```
System.out.println(MyClass.greetings);
MyClass.displayGreetings();
```

If you run the code above, you will get the following output

```
Hello World
Message = Hello World
Good morning
Greeting = Good morning
```

This is the main difference between a static field/method vs a non static field/method. For the former, you do not have to create an object to access it; you use the name of the class itself. For the latter, an object is necessary.

Some of the pre-written methods in Java are declared as static. An example is the methods in the `Arrays` class. To access the methods in this class, we use the name of the class. For instance, to use the `sort()` method, we write `Arrays.sort()`.

7.5 Advanced Methods Concepts

7.5.1 Using Arrays in Method

Before we end this chapter, I would like to discuss two more concepts about methods. The first is regarding using arrays in methods.

Previously, we learned how to use primitive data types like `int` as parameters to a method. In addition to using primitive data types, we can also use arrays.

To use an array as a parameter, we add a square bracket [] after the parameter's data type in the method declaration. An example is shown below.

```
public void printFirstElement(int[] a)
{

}
```

To call this method, we need to declare an array and pass it in as an argument to the method. We'll see an example of this later.

In addition to using arrays as parameters, we can also return an array from a method. To return an array from a method, we add a square bracket [] after the return type in the method declaration. An example is

```
public int[] returnArray()
{
    int[] a = new int[3];

    //Some code for updating values in the array

    return a;
}
```

To use this method, we need to declare an array and assign the method's result to it.

To fully understand how we can use arrays in methods, let's create a new Java application called *ArrayMethodDemo* and replace the code with the following:

```
1 package arraymethoddemo;
2
3 import java.util.Arrays;
4
5 class MyClass{
6
7   public void printFirstElement(int[] a)
8   {
9       System.out.println("The first element is " +
a[0]);
10  }
11
12  public int[] returnArray()
13  {
14     int[] a = new int[3];
15     for (int i = 0; i < a.length; i++)
16     {
17         a[i] = i*2;
18     }
19     return a;
20  }
21
22 }
23
24 public class ArrayMethodDemo {
25  public static void main(String[] args) {
26
27     MyClass amd = new MyClass();
28
29     int[] myArray = {1, 2, 3, 4, 5};
```

```
30        amd.printFirstElement(myArray);
31
32        int[] myArray2 = amd.returnArray();
33        System.out.println(Arrays.toString(myArray2));
34
35   }
36 }
```

In this example, we included two classes – `MyClass` and `ArrayMethodDemo` – in the same file again for simplicity.

Inside the class `MyClass` (lines 5 to 22), we have two methods.

The first method `printFirstElement()` shows how you can use an array as a parameter.

The second method `returnArray()` shows how you can return an array from a method.

To use these two methods, we initialized a `MyClass` object called `amd` in the `main()` method (line 27).

We then declared an array and passed it in as an argument to the `printFirstElement()` method on lines 29 and 30.

```
int[] myArray = {1, 2, 3, 4, 5};
amd.printFirstElement(myArray);
```

In addition, we also declared a second array in the `main()` method and assigned the result of the `returnArray()` method to it on line 32.

```
int[] myArray2 = amd.returnArray();
```

Finally, on line 33, we printed the contents of the array.

If you run the program above, you'll get the following output:

```
The first element is 1
[0, 2, 4]
```

7.5.2 Passing Primitive Type vs Reference Type Parameters

Now that you know how to pass an array to a method, let us look at the difference between a primitive type parameter vs a reference type parameter (such as an array). There is an important difference.

When you pass in a primitive type variable, any change made to the value of that variable is only valid within the method itself. Once the program exits the method, the change is no longer valid.

On the other hand, when you pass in a reference type variable, any change made to the value of that variable is valid even after the method ends.

To understand how this works, add the following two methods to `MyClass` in *ArrayMethodDemo.java*.

```
public void passPrimitive(int primitivePara)
{
    primitivePara = 10;
    System.out.println("Value inside method = " +
primitivePara);
}

public void passReference(int[] refPara)
{
    refPara[1] = 5;
    System.out.println("Value inside method = " +
refPara[1]);
}
```

The first method has a primitive type parameter (`int primitivePara`) and tries to change the value of that parameter. It then prints the value of the parameter.

The second method has a reference type parameter (an array) and tries to change the value of the second element in the array. It then prints the value of that element.

In our `main()` program, add the following lines of code:

```
int number = 2;
System.out.println("number before = " + number);
amd.passPrimitive(number);
System.out.println("number after = " + number);

System.out.print("\n");

System.out.println("myArray[1] before = " +
myArray[1]);
amd.passReference(myArray);
System.out.println("myArray[1] after = " +
myArray[1]);
```

If you run the program, you will get the following additional output

```
number before = 2
Value inside method = 10
number after = 2

myArray[1] before = 2
Value inside method = 5
myArray[1] after = 5
```

As you can see, the value of `number` stays the same before and after the method call. On the other hand, the value of `myArray[1]` changes after the method call.

The reason for this is because when you pass in a reference type variable, you are passing in the address of the variable. The compiler can go to the address that you passed in and make the relevant changes to the variable.

On the other hand, when you pass in a primitive type variable, you are passing in <u>the value of the variable and not the address</u>.

For instance, if the value of `number` is 2, writing

```
amd.passPrimitive(number);
```

is the same as writing

```
amd.passPrimitive(2);
```

This value 2 is assigned to the parameter `primitivePara`. Since we are not passing in the address of `number`, any change that occurs inside the method does not affect `number`.

This is an important difference that you have to understand when you pass in a primitive type variable (e.g. `int`, `float` etc) vs a reference type variable (such as an array) to a method.

Chapter 8: Object-Oriented Programming Part 2

Now, let us move on to some of the more advanced topics in object-oriented programming. In this chapter, we'll learn about inheritance, polymorphism, abstract classes and interfaces.

8.1 Inheritance

Inheritance is one of the key concepts in object-oriented programming. Simply stated, inheritance allows us to create a new class from an existing class so that we can effectively reuse existing code. In fact, all classes in Java are inherited from a pre-written base class known as the `Object` class.

The `Object` class consists of a number of pre-written methods that we can use whenever we work with classes. One such method is the `toString()` method that returns a string that represents the object. We used the `toString()` method previously when we discussed arrays. We'll be looking at the `toString()` method again when we work on our project.

So what exactly is inheritance?

8.1.1 Writing the Parent Class

Let us work through a small program together to illustrate the concept of inheritance.

Suppose we are writing a program for a fitness club that has two types of membership – VIP and Normal. To do that, let's launch NetBeans and create a new Java Project called *InheritanceDemo*.

Add a new class called `Member` to the `inheritancedemo` package. Refer to Chapter 7.2 for instructions on how to add a new class if necessary.

We'll be getting user input in the `Member` class. Hence, we need to add the statement

```
import java.util.Scanner;
```

to our class. Add this statement after the line

```
package inheritancedemo;
```

Now, we are ready to start working on the class. Add the following lines to the `Member` class (inside the curly braces).

```
public String welcome = "Welcome to ABC Fitness";
protected double annualFee;
private String name;
private int memberID;
private int memberSince;
private int discount;
```

Here, we declare six fields for the `Member` class.

The first is a public field that stores a welcome message. We initialise this field with the string "Welcome to ABC Fitness".

The other five fields include one protected field and four private fields. We'll talk more about protected fields in a later section. For now, just know that a protected field is accessible within the class in which it is declared, any class that is derived from it and any class that is in the same package. Derived classes will be covered in the next section.

Next, let's add two constructors to our class.

```java
public Member()
{
    System.out.println("Parent Constructor with no
parameter");
}

public Member(String pName, int pMemberID, int
pMemberSince)
{
    System.out.println("Parent Constructor with 3
parameters");

    name = pName;
    memberID = pMemberID;
    memberSince = pMemberSince;
}
```

The first constructor merely prints the line "Parent Constructor with no parameter".

The second constructor is more interesting. It prints the line "Parent Constructor with 3 parameters" and assigns its parameters to three of the private fields in the `Member` class.

After writing the constructors, we'll move on to the getter and setter methods. We'll add a getter and setter method for the private field `discount` so that other classes can access this field.

```java
public double getDiscount(){

    return discount;
}

public void setDiscount(){

    Scanner input = new Scanner(System.in);
    String password;
```

```java
    System.out.print("Please enter the admin
password: ");
    password = input.nextLine();

    if (!password.equals("abcd"))
    {
        System.out.println("Invalid password. You do
not have authority to edit the discount.");
    }else
    {
        System.out.print("Please enter the discount:
");
        discount = input.nextInt();
    }
}
```

The getter method simply returns the value of the `discount` field.

The setter method is more complex. It prompts the user to enter the admin password before he/she can edit the `discount` field. This method demonstrates how a setter method can be used to prevent unauthorised access to a private field. However, suffice to say, this code will be way too easy for a hacker to crack. In real life, you'll need stronger security measures than just a simple password to protect your data.

Now, let us add two more methods to our `Member` class.

The first method is a public method called `displayMemInfo()`. It uses a series of `println()` statements to display information about a member.

```java
public void displayMemInfo(){

    System.out.println("Member Name: " + name);
    System.out.println("Member ID: " + memberID);
    System.out.println("Member Since " +
memberSince);
```

```
        System.out.println("Annual Fee: " + annualFee);
}
```

The second method is a public method called
`calculateAnnualFee()`. It will be used to calculate the annual fee of
a member.

```
public void calculateAnnualFee()
{
    annualFee = 0;
}
```

Notice that we set the annual fee of a member to zero? Don't worry
about this at the moment; we'll update this method later.

Once we are done with the above, the Member class is complete.

8.1.2 Writing the Child Class

Now that we have completed the Member class, let us learn how to
derive a class from it. Derived classes are known as child classes or
subclasses, while the classes from which they are derived are known as
parent classes, base classes or superclasses.

To recap, our parent class (Member) has the following contents:

Fields

```
public String welcome = "Welcome to ABC Fitness";
protected double annualFee;
private String name;
private int memberID;
private int memberSince;
private int discount;
```

Constructors

```
public Member()
public Member(String pName, int pMemberID, int
pMemberSince)
```

Methods

```
public double getDiscount()
public void setDiscount()
public void displayMemInfo()
public void calculateAnnualFee()
```

We shall derive two classes – `NormalMember` and `VIPMember` – from the `Member` class.

First, let's declare the child class `NormalMember`.

Add a new Java class to the `inheritancedemo` package and name it `NormalMember`. Notice that when you generate a new class, NetBeans automatically declares the class as

```
public class NormalMember {

}
```

for you?

We need to indicate that `NormalMember` is derived from the `Member` class by adding the words `extends Member` to the class declaration as shown below:

```
public class NormalMember extends Member{

}
```

`extends` is a Java keyword used to indicate that one class is inherited from another class. In our example, the `NormalMember` class is inherited from the `Member` class.

We have to use the `extends` keyword whenever we want to show that one class is inherited from another class. The only exception is when inheriting from the `Object` class. As all classes in Java are inherited from the `Object` class, there is no need for us to state this inheritance explicitly.

When one class is inherited from another class, it **inherits all the public and protected fields and methods** from the parent class. This means that the child class can use these fields and methods as if they are part of its own code; we do not have to declare these fields and methods again in the child class. In other words, even though we have not started coding our child class yet, it already has two fields (`welcome` and `annualFee`) and four methods (`getDiscount`, `setDiscount`, `displayMemInfo` and `calculateAnnualFee`) inherited from the parent class. This facilitates code reuse and is especially valuable if the parent class has a large number of public/protected fields and methods that the child class can use.

However, the child class **does not inherit the private fields and methods** of the parent class. This means that the child class will not be able to access these private fields and methods directly, it'll have to access them using other methods. We'll see an example of this later.

Now that we have declared `NormalMember` as a child class of `Member`, we need to write the constructor for the child class.

Whenever we write the child class constructor, it is a must for us to call the parent class' constructor first. If we do not do that, Java will automatically call the parameterless constructor in the parent class for us.

For instance, add the following constructor to the `NormalMember` class.

```
public NormalMember() {
    System.out.println("Child constructor with no
parameter");
}
```

When we declare our constructor as above, Java looks for a parameterless constructor (i.e. a constructor with no parameter) in the parent class and calls that first before executing the code in the child constructor. If you use this constructor to create a child object, the following two lines will be displayed on the screen

```
Parent Constructor with no parameter
Child constructor with no parameter
```

The first line is from the parent constructor while the second line is from the child constructor.

If you want to call a <u>non parameterless</u> constructor in the parent class, you have to use the `super` keyword. An example is shown below:

```
public NormalMember(String pName, int pMemberID, int
pMemberSince)
{
    super(pName, pMemberID, pMemberSince);
    System.out.println("Child Constructor with 3
parameters");
}
```

When we use the `super` keyword to call a non parameterless constructor in the parent class, the statement

```
super(pName, pMemberID, pMemberSince);
```

must be the first statement in the child constructor. If we fail to do that, Java will give us an error.

In the example above, we used the `super` keyword to call the second constructor in the parent class (i.e. the constructor with 3 parameters). We passed in the values of `pName`, `pMember` and `pMemberSince` to the parent constructor.

When we create a child object with this constructor, we write something like

```
NormalMember myChildMember = new
NormalMember("James", 1, 2010);
```

You will get the following output when you run the code

```
Parent Constructor with 3 parameters
Child Constructor with 3 parameters
```

Behind the scene, the values "James", 1 and 2010 are assigned to the fields `name`, `memberID` and `memberSince` respectively.

At this point, some of you may be wondering where the fields `name`, `memberID` and `memberSince` come from? Since these are private fields in the `Member` class and we mentioned that private fields are not inherited, why would the child class have these fields?

The reason for this is that when we say private fields are not inherited, it simply means the child class cannot access these fields directly. However, these fields do exist in the child class. The only difference is that the child class cannot access them directly but has to use constructors or setter and getter methods instead. We'll see an example of how we can use getter and setter methods to access these private fields later.

Overriding a Method

Now that we have created the constructors for our child class, let us move on to create a method to calculate the annual fee of a normal member. Recall that we have already coded a `calculateAnnualFee()` method in the parent class earlier? As this parent class method is `public`, it is inherited by the child class. Hence, the child class can use this method as if it is part of its own code.

However, recall that the `calculateAnnualFee()` method in the parent class sets the annual fee of a member to zero? What if we want to use a different formula for calculating the annual fee in the child class? In this case, we have to override the inherited method.

Overriding a method simply means writing a new version of the method in the child class.

To override the `calculateAnnualFee()` method, add the following code to the `NormalMember` class.

```
@Override
public void calculateAnnualFee()
{
    annualFee = (1-0.01*discount)*(100 + 12*30);
}
```

Notice that there is a red squiggly line under the word `discount` when you save your code? This indicates an error. If you hover your mouse over the line, you'll get the message "discount has private access in Member". This is because `discount` is a private field in `Member` and is thus not accessible directly by `NormalMember`.

In order for `NormalMember` to access the `discount` field, we have to use the getter method declared in `Member`. Change the code above to

```
annualFee = (1-0.01*getDiscount())*(100 + 12*30);
```

Once you replace `discount` with `getDiscount()`, the error goes away.

Annotations

Next, notice the `@Override` line above the method declaration? This is known as an annotation. In Java, annotations are metadata that we add to our code to provide extra information to the compiler.

When we use the `@Override` annotation, we are informing the compiler that the method that follows is meant to override the `calculateAnnualFee()` method declared in the base class (i.e. the `Member` class).

When overriding a method, there are some rules that we must follow. For instance, the method in the child class must have the same parameter list as the method in the parent class. If the method in the child class fails to override the method in the parent class correctly, the compiler will generate an error. If that happens, you can hover your mouse over the error for more information.

Using the `@Override` annotation is optional when overriding a method. However, you are strongly encouraged to do so to prevent compilation errors.

Annotations follow a fixed syntax and are case sensitive. `@override`, `@overriding` or `@ThisMethodOverrideAnother` are all invalid annotations. Java comes with a number of predefined annotations. You can find the full list of predefined annotations here https://docs.oracle.com/javase/tutorial/java/annotations/predefined.html.

That's all for our child class `NormalMember`. The class has the following contents:

Fields

Inherited from parent class:
```
public String welcome = "Welcome to ABC Fitness";
protected double annualFee
```

Constructors

```
public NormalMember()
public NormalMember(String pName, int pMemberID, int
pMemberSince)
```

Methods

Inherited from parent class:
```
public void setDiscount()
public double getDiscount()
public void displayMemInfo()
```

Overriden in child class:
```
public void calculateAnnualFee()
```

Next, we shall add another class – VIPMember – to our inheritance package. This class also inherits from Member. To do that, add a new class to the inheritancedemo package and name it VIPMember. Replace the code with the code below:

```
package inheritancedemo;

public class VIPMember extends Member {

    public VIPMember(String pName, int pMemberID, int
pMemberSince)
    {
        super(pName, pMemberID, pMemberSince);
        System.out.println("Child Constructor with 3
parameters");
    }

    @Override
    public void calculateAnnualFee()
    {
        annualFee = (1-0.01*getDiscount())*1200;
```

```
        }
}
```

This class has one constructor (with 3 parameters) and one method `calculateAnnualFee()`. The `calculateAnnualFee()` method here uses a different formula for calculating annual fee from the `calculateAnnualFee()` method in the `NormalMember` class. It is alright for the two methods to share the same name (and signature) as they are in different classes.

`VIPMember` class has the following contents:

Fields

Inherited from parent class:
```
public String welcome = "Welcome to ABC Fitness";
protected double annualFee
```

Constructors

```
public VIPMember(String pName, int pMemberID, int pMemberSince)
```

Methods

Inherited from parent class:
```
public void setDiscount()
public double getDiscount()
public void displayMemInfo()
```

Overridden in child class:
```
public void calculateAnnualFee()
```

8.1.3 The main() method

Now that we have written the three classes that we need, let's write the code for the `main()` method. Switch over to the *InheritanceDemo.java* file and add the following two lines to the `main()` method.

```
NormalMember mem1 = new NormalMember("James", 1,
2010);
VIPMember mem2 = new VIPMember("Andy", 2, 2011);
```

Here, we are creating two objects for the two derived classes.

`mem1` is created using the 3 parameters constructor from the `NormalMember` class.
`mem2` is created using the 3 parameters constructor from the `VIPMember` class.

Now we'll use the `calculateAnnualFee()` methods in the respective classes to calculate the annual fee for each member.

```
mem1.calculateAnnualFee();
mem2.calculateAnnualFee();
```

As `mem1` is an instance of the `NormalMember` class, the `calculateAnnualFee()` method from that class is executed. The annual fee for `mem1` is thus 100 + 12*30 = 460. For `mem2`, the annual fee is 1200 as it uses the method from the `VIPMember` class.

Finally, let's use the `displayMemberInfo()` method from the parent class (`Member`) to display the information on our screen. We write

```
mem1.displayMemInfo();
mem2.displayMemInfo();
```

Since the `displayMemberInfo()` method belongs to the parent class and is `public`, both `mem1` and `mem2` have inherited the method and are thus able to use it in the `main()` method.

You'll get the following output when you run the program:

```
Parent Constructor with 3 parameters
Child Constructor with 3 parameters
Parent Constructor with 3 parameters
Child Constructor with 3 parameters
Member Name: James
Member ID: 1
Member Since 2010
Annual Fee: 460.0
Member Name: Andy
Member ID: 2
Member Since 2011
Annual Fee: 1200.0
```

Now, we shall try to apply some discount to the annual fees for `mem1`. As `discount` is a private field in the parent class, we cannot alter its value by writing something like

```
mem1.discount = 100;
```

Instead, we have to use the `setDiscount()` method. To do that, add the following line to the `main()` method.

```
mem1.setDiscount();
```

Next, we'll add the following statements to recalculate the annual fee after the discount and display the information.

```
mem1.calculateAnnualFee();
mem1.displayMemInfo();
```

Run the program again. When prompted, enter "abcd" for password and 30 for discount. You'll get the following lines added to the original output.

```
Please enter the admin password: abcd
Please enter the discount: 30
Member Name: James
Member ID: 1
```

```
Member Since 2010
Annual Fee: 322.0
```

The annual fee is now 322 because a discount of 30% is applied.

8.2 Polymorphism

Now that we have seen an example of how inheritance works, let us move on to discuss another topic that is closely related to inheritance - the concept of polymorphism. Polymorphism refers to a program's ability to use the correct method for an object based on its run-time type.

The best way to explain polymorphism is through an example. Let's expand on our fitness club example above.

First, delete or comment out all the code in the previous `main()` method and add the following lines to it.

```
Member[] clubMembers = new Member[6];

clubMembers[0] = new NormalMember("James", 1, 2010);
clubMembers[1] = new NormalMember("Andy", 2, 2011);
clubMembers[2] = new NormalMember("Bill", 3, 2011);
clubMembers[3] = new VIPMember("Carol", 4, 2012);
clubMembers[4] = new VIPMember("Evelyn", 5, 2012);
clubMembers[5] = new Member("Yvonne", 6, 2013);
```

Here, we declare an array of `Member` objects and add 6 members to it. The first three members are objects of the `NormalMember` class, the next two are objects of the `VIPMember` class while the last is an object of the `Member` class.

Although `clubMembers` is declared to be an array of `Member` type, we can assign objects of `NormalMember` and `VIPMember` to it as they are child classes of the `Member` class. We do not need to declare separate arrays for `NormalMember` and `VIPMember` objects.

Next, we'll use an enhanced `for` statement to calculate the annual fee of each member and display the information.

To do that, we write

```
for (Member m : clubMembers)
{
    m.calculateAnnualFee();
    m.displayMemInfo();
}
```

Now save and run the program. You'll notice that the annual fee for the first three members (`NormalMember`) is $460, the annual fee for the next two (`VIPMember`) is $1200 and the annual fee for the last member is $0.

This is the result of polymorphism. At run time (i.e. when the program runs), the program determines that the first three members of `clubMembers` are of `NormalMember` type and executes the `calculateAnnualFee()` method from that class. It also determines that the next two members are of `VIPMember` type and executes the method from that class. Finally, it determines that the last member is of `Member` type and executes the method from the parent class.

We say that the runtime type of the first three elements of `clubMembers` is `NormalMember`, the runtime type of the next two is `VIPMember` and the runtime type of the last element is `Member`. In contrast, the declared type of all the 5 elements is `Member`.

Polymorphism simply means that at run time, although all objects are declared to be of `Member` type, the program is smart enough to use the correct `calculateAnnualFee()` method based on the runtime type of the element.

8.3 Abstract Classes and Methods

Next, let us move on to discuss two special types of "parent class" in Java - abstract classes and interfaces.

We'll first look at abstract classes.

An abstract class is a special type of class that is created strictly to be a base class for other classes to derive from. They cannot be instantiated. In other words, if `FourWheelVehicles` is an abstract class, the statement

```
FourWheelVehicle myVeh = new FourWheelVehicle();
```

will give you an error as you cannot create an object of an abstract class.

Abstract classes may have fields and methods just like any other classes. In addition, they can have a special type of method known as abstract methods. <u>Abstract methods are methods that have no body and MUST be implemented in the derived class</u>. They can only exist in abstract classes.

In the fitness club example above, we declared a method called `calculateAnnualFee()` in the parent class (`Member`) and set the annual fee to zero. This method does not make any logical sense as the annual fee is zero.

Instead of adding such senseless method implementations in our parent class, a better way would be to declare the method as an abstract method.

Let's see how we can do that in our fitness club example. We're going to have to make some changes to our program.

Changes to the parent class

First, we need to replace the lines

```
public void calculateAnnualFee()
{
    annualFee = 0;
}
```

in the `Member` class with

```
abstract public void calculateAnnualFee();
```

We add the `abstract` keyword in the method declaration above to indicate that this is an abstract method. In addition, we do not add braces { } after the method declaration as abstract methods have no body. Instead, we end the declaration with a semi-colon (;).

Next, we need to declare our `Member` class as an abstract class. This is because abstract methods can only exist in abstract classes.

To do that, we add the `abstract` keyword to the `Member` class declaration like this:

```
abstract public class Member
```

That's all the changes that we need to make to the `Member` class.

Changes to the InheritanceDemo class

Next, we need to make one change to the `InheritanceDemo` class.

As abstract classes cannot be instantiated, the line

```
clubMembers[5] = new Member("Yvonne", 6, 2013);
```

in the *InheritanceDemo.java* file will give us an error.

To remedy that, we can change the last item in our `clubMember` array to either a `NormalMember` or a `VIPMember` object. This works well with the logic of our program as a member should either be a `NormalMember` or a `VIPMember`, not just a `Member`.

In our example, we'll change the item to a `VIPMember` object.

Change the line to

```
clubMembers[5] = new VIPMember("Yvonne", 6, 2013);
```

That's all there is for the `InheritanceDemo` class.

Changes to the sub classes

Finally, let's move on to the subclasses. As abstract methods have to be implemented by subclasses, we need to ensure that we have implemented the `calculateAnnualFee()` method in both our subclasses.

In our previous example, we have already implemented this method in both of the subclasses. Hence, we do not need to make any changes to the subclasses.

We are now ready to save and run the program. Everything should run normally as before except for the output for last member (Yvonne). The annual fee should now be $1200 as shown below.

```
Member Name: Yvonne
Member ID: 6
Member Since 2013
Annual Fee: 1200.0
```

This is the gist of abstract classes. In summary, an abstract class is a special type of base class that cannot be instantiated. It can contain abstract methods that have no implementation details and MUST be implemented in the child class.

8.4 Interfaces

Next, let's look at interfaces. Interfaces are much like abstract classes in that they cannot be instantiated. Instead, they must be implemented by classes or extended by other interfaces. When a class implements an interface, it has to implement all the abstract methods in that interface.

Up until Java 7, interfaces can only contain abstract methods (i.e. methods with no bodies) and constants (i.e. fields declared as `final`). All methods in an interface are implicitly `public` while all constant values are implicitly `public`, `static`, and `final`. You do not have to specify these modifiers.

One of the key differences between an abstract class and an interface is that a class can only extend one abstract class but can implement multiple interfaces. However, we won't be showing an example of multiple interfaces implementation in this book as that is an advanced topic beyond the scope of the book.

Another difference between an abstract class and an interface is that an interface can only contain abstract methods (up until Java 7) while an abstract class can contain non-abstract methods.

Let us first look at an example of how interface works up until Java 7.

Launch NetBeans and create a new Java Project called *InterfaceDemo*. Replace the code in *InterfaceDemo.java* with the following:

```
1 package interfacedemo;
2
3 public class InterfaceDemo {
4
5    public static void main(String[] args) {
6       MyClass a = new MyClass();
7       a.someMethod();
8
```

```
9      System.out.println("The value of the constant
is " + MyInterface.myInt);
10  }
11 }
12
13 class MyClass implements MyInterface
14 {
15   @Override
16   public void someMethod()
17   {
18      System.out.println("This is a method
implemented in MyClass");
19   }
20 }
21
22 interface MyInterface{
23
24   int myInt = 5;
25   void someMethod();
26
27 }
```

In the example above, the interface is declared on lines 22 to 27. On line 24, we declared a field (which is implicitly `public`, `static` and `final`) and on line 25, we declared a method. There is no need to use the `abstract` keyword when declaring a method in an interface. It is abstract by default.

On lines 13 to 20, we have a class called `MyClass` that implements the interface. We use the `implement` keyword to indicate this relationship. Inside the class, we implement the method `someMethod()` from line 15 to 19.

From line 3 to 11, we have the `InterfaceDemo` class which contains the `main()` method. Inside the `main()` method, we instantiated a `MyClass` object and use that to invoke `someMethod()` on line 7. On line 9, we printed out the value of the constant `myInt`. Note that because constants in interfaces are `static`, we access them using the name of the interface (`MyInterface.myInt`) and not the name of the `MyClass` object.

If you run this program, you'll get

```
This is a method implemented in MyClass
The value of the constant is 5
```

The example above shows a simple example of how interfaces work up until Java 7. However, things changed a bit in Java 8.

Prior to Java 8, an interface can only contain abstract methods. In Java 8, Java added support for default and static methods in interfaces.

To see how default and static methods work, add the following two methods to `MyInterface`. Note that both methods are implemented in the interface itself.

```java
public static void someStaticMethod()
{
    System.out.println("This is a static method in an interface");
}

public default void someDefaultMethod()
{
    System.out.println("This is a default method in an interface");
}
```

Next, add the following lines to the `main()` method.

```java
a.someDefaultMethod();
MyInterface.someStaticMethod();
```

Now, save and run the program. You'll get the following output:

```
This is a method implemented in MyClass
The value of the constant is 5
This is a default method in an interface
This is a static method in an interface
```

This is how interfaces work from Java 8 onwards. We are now allowed to add method implementations in our interfaces. However, only default and static methods can be implemented in an interface.

Java added default and static methods in interfaces mainly to ensure binary compatibility. Simply stated, binary compatibility means that when you change your interface, you do not need to make any changes to the classes that implement it.

For instance, suppose we want to add a new method to our interface MyInterface. If we simply add the method declaration to the interface as shown below, we will get an error.

```
interface MyInterface{

    int myInt = 5;
    void someMethod();
    void someNewMethod();
}
```

This is because the class that implements this interface (MyClass) did not implement the new method. A class that implements an interface must implement all the abstract methods in the interface. Hence, if you add an abstract method to your interface, you need to ensure that all classes that implement your interface implement the new method. This is often impossible to do as you may have no idea which classes implemented your interface.

To overcome this problem, Java added support for default and static methods for interfaces. This allows us to add methods to our interfaces without having to make any changes to the classes that implemented it.

8.5 Access Modifiers Revisited

Now that we have covered various topics related to inheritance, let us take a second look at the concept of access modifiers in object oriented programming. Earlier, we learnt that an access modifier is like a gatekeeper. It controls who has access to a certain field or method. Java comes with 3 access modifiers: `private`, `public` and `protected`. If an access modifier is not stated, the access level is taken to be package-private.

To understand how `private`, `public`, `protected` and package-private work, let's consider the example below. We'll be using fields to demonstrate the concept. The same applies to methods.

Create a new NetBeans project and name it *ModifierDemo*. Replace the code in *ModiferDemo.java* with the following

```
package modifierdemo;

public class ModifierDemo {

    public int publicNum = 2;
    protected int protectedNum = 3;
    int packagePrivateNum = 4;
    private int privateNum = 1;

}
```

Now create another class in the modifierdemo package and name it ClassesInSamePackage. Replace the code in *ClassesInSamePackage.java* with the following

```
package modifierdemo;

public class ClassesInSamePackage
{
    //just an empty class
```

```
}

class ClassA extends ModifierDemo
{
    public void printMessages()
    {
      //This is ok
      System.out.println(publicNum);

      //This is ok
      System.out.println(protectedNum);

      //This is ok
      System.out.println(packagePrivateNum);

      //This is NOT ok
      System.out.println(privateNum);
    }
}

class ClassB
{
    public void printMessages()
    {

      ModifierDemo p = new ModifierDemo();

      //This is ok
      System.out.println(p.publicNum);

      //This is ok
      System.out.println(p.protectedNum);

      //This is ok
      System.out.println(p.packagePrivateNum);

      //This is NOT ok
```

```
      System.out.println(p.privateNum);
   }
}
```

In the code above, we added two classes to the *ClassesInSamePackage.java* file. `ClassA` extends the `ModifierDemo` class while `ClassB` does not.

In `ClassA`, the first two `println()` statements will not give us any error as a derived class can access any public and protected fields in the parent class. In addition, the third `println()` statement will also not give us an error as both files (*ModifierDemo.java* and *ClassesInSamePackage.java*) are inside the same package. By default, a field declared without any access modifier is package-private. A package-private field is accessible to all files in the same package.

However, the fourth statement gives us an error as `privateNum` is a private field and is thus only accessible in `ModifierDemo` itself.

In `ClassB`, as the class is not derived from `ModifierDemo`, we need to instantiate a `ModifierDemo` object `p` in order to access the fields of `ModifierDemo`.

As before, the first and third `println()` statements do not give us any error. This is because a public field can be accessed by any class while a package-private field can be accessed by any class in the same package.

The second `println()` statements also does not give us any errors. Even though `ClassB` is not derived from `ModifierDemo`, it can access `protectedNum` as protected fields are not only accessible to all subclasses of the class in which they are declared, they are also accessible to all classes in the same package (similar to package-private).

The fourth `println()` statement gives us an error as a private field is only accessible in the class that it is declared.

Now, let's look at what happens when two classes are not in the same package. Create a new package for the project.

To do that, right click on the project name in the Project Explorer and select **New** > **Java Package…** (refer to image below). Name this package `anotherpackage`.

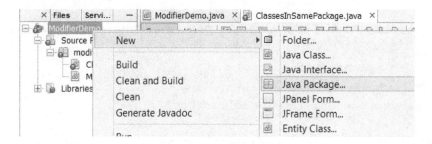

When you create a new package for the *ModifierDemo* project, you are essentially creating a sub-folder under the main project folder.

If you browse to the main project folder now, you'll see two sub-folders created – one for the default package `modifierdemo` (which was created by NetBeans when you created the project) and the other for the newly created package, `anotherpackage`. If you can't find the main folder, you can right-click on the project name in the Project Explorer in NetBeans and select **Properties**. This will bring up a dialogue box that shows where your project is stored.

Now, add a new class to this package. To do that, right-click on the `anotherpackage` package in the Project explorer and select **New > Java Class…** You may need to click on the + sign in the Project Explorer if you do not see this package. It is very important that you click on the correct package when creating a new class in NetBeans.

Name this class `ClassesInAnotherPackage`. If you have done it correctly, you should see the following structure in your Project explorer.

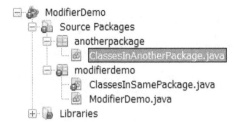

Replace the code in *ClassesInAnotherPackage.java* with the following:

```
package anotherpackage;

import modifierdemo.ModifierDemo;

public class ClassesInAnotherPackage
{
    //just an empty class
}

class MyClassC extends ModifierDemo{
    public void printMessages()
    {

        //This is ok
        System.out.println(publicNum);

        //This is ok
        System.out.println(protectedNum);

        //This is NOT ok
        System.out.println(packagePrivateNum);

        //This is NOT ok
        System.out.println(privateNum);
    }
}
```

```
class MyClassD {

    public void printMessages()
    {
        ModifierDemo p = new ModifierDemo();

        //This is ok
        System.out.println(p.publicNum);

        //This is NOT ok
        System.out.println(p.protectedNum);

        //This is NOT ok
        System.out.println(p.packagePrivateNum);

        //This is NOT ok
        System.out.println(p.privateNum);
    }
}
```

In the example above, `ClassC` can access `publicNum` and `protectedNum` but not `packagePrivateNum` and `privateNum`. It can access `protectedNum` because it is a child class of `ModifierDemo` even though it is not in the same package as `ModifierDemo`. On the other hand, it cannot access `packagePrivateNum` because this field is only accessible by classes in the same package as `ModifierDemo`.

Next, for `ClassD`, it can only access `publicNum`. It cannot access `protectedNum` as it is neither a subclass of `ModifierDemo` nor in the same package. Similarly, it cannot access `packagePrivateNum` and `privateNum`.

In short, anything that is declared as `public` is accessible everywhere; there are no restrictions on accessing public fields. On the other hand, anything declared as `private` is only accessible within the class in which it is declared. Anything declared as `protected` is accessible within the class in which it is declared, any class that is derived from it and any class that is in the same package as the class that it is declared in. Finally, anything declared without an access modifier is package-private and is only accessible within the package in which it is declared.

Chapter 9: Collections

Congratulations on making it thus far. We've come a long way.

In the last two chapters, you learned how to write your own classes and instantiate objects.

In this chapter, we are going to look at a framework that Java provides to enable us to easily store and manipulate these objects. Specifically, we'll be looking at the Java Collections Framework.

9.1 The Java Collections Framework

The Java Collections Framework is a set of pre-written classes and interfaces that Java provides to help us organise and manipulate groups of objects. Using the Collections Framework, we can choose to organise our objects in different formats such as lists, sets, queues or maps.

We'll be looking at how to use lists in this chapter.

The Java Collections Framework standardizes the way in which groups of objects are handled. Hence, once you know how to use lists, you'll find it easier to learn other collections such as sets or queues.

9.2 Autoboxing and Unboxing

Before we can discuss the Java Collections Framework, we need to first discuss the concept of autoboxing and unboxing.

Previously in Chapter 3, we learned about the 8 primitive types in Java. These 8 primitive types are basic data types and not objects.

However, Java is an object-oriented language and much of language revolves around the idea of treating everything as an object. Hence, oftentimes, we find it necessary to convert a primitive type into an object.

To facilitate this conversion, Java provides us with what is known as wrapper classes. Each primitive type in Java has a corresponding wrapper class. These wrapper classes contain a number of useful methods that we can use. The wrapper classes for

`boolean, char, byte, short, int, long, float` and `double`

are

`Boolean, Character, Byte, Short, Integer, Long, Float` and `Double` respectively.

Converting from a primitive data type into a wrapper class object is easy.

For instance, to convert `int` into an `Integer` object, we do the following:

```
Integer intObject = new Integer(100);
```

Here, we declare and instantiate an `Integer` object by passing an `int` value of 100 to the `Integer` class constructor. This constructor accepts the value and creates an `Integer` object based on that value.

If we want to convert the `Integer` object back to an `int`, we use the `intValue()` method. The code is as follows:

```
int m = intObject.intValue();
```

The `intValue()` method returns an `int` type which we assign to `m`.

As you can see, converting from a primitive data type to an object and vice versa is relatively straightforward. However in practice, it is actually simpler than what is shown above. Java provides us with two mechanisms known as autoboxing and unboxing. This allows for automatic conversion.

To convert from `int` to `Integer`, instead of writing

```
Integer intObject = new Integer(100);
```

we can simply write

```
Integer intObject = 100;
```

Here, we simply assign the value 100 to `intObject`. We do not need to pass this `int` value to the `Integer` constructor; Java does it for us behind the scene. This process is known as autoboxing.

To convert from `Integer` to `int`, instead of writing

```
int m = intObject.intValue();
```

we can simply write

```
int m = intObject;
```

We do not need to explicitly use the `intValue()` method. When we assign an `Integer` object to an `int` variable, Java automatically converts the `Integer` object to `int` type. This process is known as unboxing.

As we can see, wrapper classes provide us with a convenient way to convert primitive types into objects and vice verse. Besides this purpose, wrapper classes also have another major use – they provide us with methods for converting strings into primitive types. Suppose you want to convert a string into an `int`, you can use the `parseInt()` method in the `Integer` class as shown below:

```
int n = Integer.parseInt("5");
```

Note that `"5"` is a string as we use double quotes. The `Integer.parseInt("5")` method returns the `int` value 5, which we then assign to n.

If the string cannot be converted into an `int`, the method will throw a `NumberFormatException`. For instance, the statement below will give us an error:

```
int p = Integer.parseInt("ABC");
```

In addition to converting a string into an `int`, we can also convert a string into a `double` using the `parseDouble()` method found in the `Double` class:

```
double q = Double.parseDouble("5.1");
```

Similarly, we'll get an error if the string cannot be converted into a double.

9.3 Lists

Now that we are familiar with wrapper classes, let us look at lists. A list is very similar to an array, but is more flexible. Specifically, its size can be changed.

Previously, in Chapter 4, we learned that the size of an array cannot be changed once we initialize the array or if we state the number of elements when declaring it.

For instance, if you declare the array as
```
int[] myArray = new int[10];
```

`myArray` can only hold 10 values. If you write `myArray[10]` (which refers to the 11th value since array index starts from zero), you will get an error.

If you need greater flexibility in your program, you can use a list. Java comes with a pre-written `List` interface that is part of the Java Collections Framework. This interface is implemented by a few classes.

The most commonly used classes that implement the `List` interface are the `ArrayList` and `LinkedList` classes. We'll look at `ArrayList` first.

9.4 ArrayList

The `ArrayList` class is a pre-written class that implements the `List` interface. Like all other collections in the Java Collections Framerwork, an `ArrayList` can only be used to store objects (not primitive data types). Hence, if we want to declare a list of integers, we have to use `Integer` instead of `int`.

Whenever you use an `ArrayList`, you have to import the `java.util.ArrayList` class using the statement below

```
import java.util.ArrayList;
```

The syntax for declaring and instantiating an `ArrayList` is as follows:

```
ArrayList<Type> nameOfArrayList = new ArrayList<>();
```

For instance, to declare and instantiate an `ArrayList` of `Integer` objects, we write

```
ArrayList<Integer> userAgeList = new ArrayList<>();
```

On the left side of the statement, we declared an `ArrayList` variable.

`ArrayList` is a keyword to indicate that you are declaring an `ArrayList`

`<Integer>` indicates that this `ArrayList` is used to store `Integer` objects

`userAgeList` is the name of the `ArrayList`.

On the right side, we instantiate a new `ArrayList` object using the `new` keyword and assign it to `userAgeList`.

If you want the `ArrayList` to store `String` objects instead, you declare and instantiate it as

```
ArrayList<String> userNameList = new ArrayList<>();
```

In both examples above, we specifically declared an `ArrayList` and assigned an `ArrayList` to it. However, if you prefer, you can also choose to declare a `List` instead and assign an `ArrayList` to it.

This is allowed because `List` is the superinterface of `ArrayList`.

To declare a `List` and assign an `ArrayList` to it, we write

```
List<String> userNameList2 = new ArrayList<>();
```

You need to import `java.util.List` if you do it this way.

9.4.1 ArrayList Methods

The `ArrayList` class comes with a large number of pre-written methods that we can use. All methods discussed below can be used whether you declared an `ArrayList` or you declared a `List` and assigned an `ArrayList` to it.

add()

To add members to a list, use the `add()` method.

```
userAgeList.add(40);
userAgeList.add(53);
userAgeList.add(45);
userAgeList.add(53);
```

`userAgeList` now has 4 members.

You can use `System.out.println()` to print out the members of a list. If you write

```
System.out.println(userAgeList);
```

you'll get

```
[40, 53, 45, 53]
```

as the output.

To add members at a specific position, do the following:

```
userAgeList.add(2, 51);
```

This inserts the number 51 into index 2 (i.e. the third position).

`userAgeList` now becomes `[40, 53, 51, 45, 53]`.

set()

To replace an element at a specified position with another element, use the `set()` method.

For instance, to change the element at index 3 to 49, do the following:

```
userAgeList.set(3, 49);
```

The first argument is the index of the element that you want to replace and the second argument is the value that you want to replace it with.

`userAgeList` now becomes `[40, 53, 51, 49, 53]`.

remove()

To remove member at a specific position from the list, use the `remove()` method. The `remove()` method takes in the index of the item to be removed as argument. For instance, if we write

`userAgeList.remove(3);`

The element at index 3 is removed.

`userAgeList` becomes `[40, 53, 51, 53]`.

get()

To get the element at a specific position, use the `get()` method.

`userAgeList.get(2);`

gives us the number 51.

size()

To find out the number of elements in the list, use the `size()` method.

`userAgeList.size()` gives us 4 as there are 4 elements in the `ArrayList` at the moment.

contains()

To check if a list contains a certain member, use the `contains()` method.

To check if `userAgeList` contains '51', we write

`userAgeList.contains(51);`

we will get `true` as the result.

If we write

```
userAgeList.contains(12);
```

we will get `false` as the result.

indexOf()

To get the index of the first occurrence of a certain element, use the `indexOf()` method. If the element does not exist in the `ArrayList`, the method returns -1.

For instance, if we write

```
userAgeList.indexOf(53);
```

we'll get 1 as the result. Even though 53 appears in the `ArrayList` twice, we'll only get the index of the first occurrence.

If we write

```
userAgeList.indexOf(12);
```

we'll get -1 as the number 12 does not exist in the `ArrayList`.

toArray()

To get all the elements in the `ArrayList`, use the `toArray()` method. This method returns an array of `Object` type containing all of the elements in the `ArrayList` in proper sequence (from first to last element).

For instance, we can write

```
Object[] myArray = userAgeList.toArray();
```

to convert `userAgeList` to an `Object[]` array. (Recall that the `Object` class is the parent class of all classes in Java.)

If you want `toArray()` to return a specific type of array instead, you can pass the type of array in as an argument. For instance, if you want `toArray()` to return an `Integer[]` array instead of the default `Object[]` array, you can write

```
Integer[] myIntArray = userAgeList.toArray(new
Integer[0]);
```

Here we pass an `Integer` array of size 0 (`new Integer[0]`) to the `toArray()` method.

When we do this, the `toArray()` method returns an `Integer` array which we can then assign to `myIntArray`.

clear()

To remove all items in a list, use the `clear()` method. If we write

```
userAgeList.clear();
```

we will have no elements left in the list.

For a complete list of all the `ArrayList` methods available in Java, check out this page
https://docs.oracle.com/javase/8/docs/api/java/util/ArrayList.html

9.5 LinkedList

Next, let's look at `LinkedList`.

A `LinkedList` is very similar to an `ArrayList` and is thus very similar to use. They both implement the `List` interface.

The main difference between a `LinkedList` and an `ArrayList` is their implementation. An `ArrayList` is implemented as a resizable array. As more elements are added, its size is increased dynamically. Whenever we add a new element to the middle of an `ArrayList`, all the elements after it have to be shifted. For instance, if `myArrayList` has three elements as shown below

```
myArrayList = {"Hello", "Good", "Morning"};
```

and we want to insert the string "World" into position 1 (i.e. after "Hello"), all the elements after "Hello" have to be shifted.

Similarly, when we delete an element from an `ArrayList`, all the elements after the deleted element have to be shifted up. This can result in a significant delay if the `ArrayList` is large.

If there is a need for frequent addition and deletion of elements from a `List`, it is better to use a `LinkedList`. A `LinkedList` stores the addresses of the elements before and after each element. For instance, suppose a `LinkedList` has three elements "Hello", "Good" and "Morning" at addresses 111, 122 and 133 respectively. The diagram below shows how a `LinkedList` is implemented.

As "Hello" is the first element, there is no element before it. Hence the box on the left shows an arrow pointing to `null` (`null` simply means it is pointing to nothing). The box on the right stores the address 122, which is the address of the next element.

For the element "Good", the box on the left stores the address 111 (the address of the previous element) and the box on the right stores the address 133 (the address of the next element).

Now suppose we delete the element "Good". The diagram below shows how the addresses are updated (the underlined addresses).

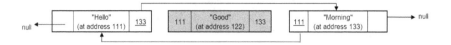

For the element "Hello", the box on the right now stores the address 133, which is the address of the element "Morning".

When the `List` is implemented as such, there is no need to shift any element when elements are added or deleted. The addresses are simply updated when necessary

Since there is now no element pointing to the element "Good", the Java Virtual Machine will eventually delete this element so as to free up any memory that it may be using.

When to use a LinkedList over an ArrayList?

Generally, we use a `LinkedList` when there is a need to add or remove elements frequently.

In addition, the `LinkedList` class implements the `Queue` and `Deque` interfaces on top of the `List` interface. `Queue` and `Deque` are two other interfaces in the Java Collections Framework. Hence, you will have to use a `LinkedList` instead of an `ArrayList` if you want to use any of the methods from these two interfaces (such as `offer()`, `peek()`, `poll()`, `getFirst()`, `getLast()` etc).

However, note that a `LinkedList` has higher memory consumption than an `ArrayList` as memory is needed to store the addresses of the neighbouring elements. It is also more time-consuming to find a specific element in a `LinkedList` as you have to start from the first element in the list and follow the references until you get to that item. This is in contrast to an `ArrayList` where the address of each element can be calculated based on the address of the first element. Therefore, it is not advisable to use a `LinkedList` if memory is a concern or if there is a frequent need to search for an element.

Now, let's look at how we can declare and instantiate a `LinkedList`. The syntax is as follows:

```
LinkedList<Type> nameOfLinkedList = new
LinkedList<>();
```

For instance, to declare and instantiate a `LinkedList` of `Integer` objects, we write

```
LinkedList<Integer> userAgeLinkedList = new
LinkedList<>();
```

This is very similar to how you declare and instantiate an `ArrayList`. The only difference is you change the word `ArrayList` to `LinkedList`. You need to import the `LinkedList` class when using a `LinkedList`. To do so, use the import statement below:

```
import java.util.LinkedList;
```

Similar to an `ArrayList`, you can also choose to declare a `List` and assign a `LinkedList` to it. To do that, you write

```
List<Integer> userAgeLinkedList2 = new
LinkedList<>();
```

If you do it this way, you need to import the `List` class too.

9.5.1 LinkedList Methods

The `LinkedList` class comes with a large number of pre-written methods that we can use. However, as both the `LinkedList` and `ArrayList` classes implement the `List` interface, they share a lot of the same methods. In fact, all the methods covered in the `ArrayList` section can be used with a `LinkedList`.

That means you can use the `add()`, `set()`, `get()`, `size()`, `remove()`, `contains()`, `indexOf()`, `toArray()` and `clear()` methods in the same way for both `ArrayList` and `LinkedList`. To appreciate this fact, launch NetBeans and start a new Project called *ListDemo*.

Replace the code with the code below:

```
package listdemo;
import java.util.ArrayList;
import java.util.LinkedList;
import java.util.List;

public class ListDemo {

    public static void main(String[] args) {

        List<Integer> userAgeList = new ArrayList<>();

        userAgeList.add(40);
        userAgeList.add(53);
        userAgeList.add(45);
        userAgeList.add(53);
        userAgeList.add(2, 51);

        System.out.println(userAgeList.size());
        userAgeList.remove(3);
        System.out.println(userAgeList.contains(12));
        System.out.println(userAgeList.indexOf(12));
        System.out.println(userAgeList.get(2));

        Integer[] userAgeArray =
userAgeList.toArray(new Integer[0]);
        System.out.println(userAgeArray[0]);
```

```
        System.out.println(userAgeList);
    }
}
```

This code demonstrates some of the methods mentioned in the
`ArrayList` section. If you run the code, you'll get

```
5
false
-1
51
40
[40, 53, 51, 53]
```

Now, change the statement

```
List<Integer> userAgeList = new ArrayList<>();
```

to

```
List<Integer> userAgeList = new LinkedList<>();
```

and run the program again.

What do you notice? Everything runs perfectly and you get the same
output right?

That's because both the `ArrayList` class and `LinkedList` class
implement the `List` interface. Hence a lot of methods are common to
both classes.

However, as mentioned above, in addition to implementing the `List`
interface, the `LinkedList` class also implements the `Queue` and `Deque`
interface. Therefore, it has some additional methods that are missing in
the `List` interface and the `ArrayList` class.

If you want to use these methods, you have to specifically declare a `LinkedList` instead of a `List`. Change the statement

```
List<Integer> userAgeList = new LinkedList<>();
```

to

```
LinkedList<Integer> userAgeList = new LinkedList<>();
```

to try the methods below.

poll()

The `poll()` method returns the first element (also known as the head) of the list and removes the element from the list. It returns `null` if the list is empty.

If `userAgeList` is currently `[40, 53, 51, 53]` and you write

```
System.out.println(userAgeList.poll());
```

you'll get

```
40
```

as the output since the first element in `userAgeList` is 40. If you print out the elements of the `userAgeList` again, you'll get

```
[53, 51, 53].
```

The first element is removed from the list.

peek()

The `peek()` method is similar to the `poll()` method. It returns the first element of the list but does not remove the element from the list. It returns `null` if the list is empty.

getFirst()

The `getFirst()` method is almost identical to the `peek()` method. It returns the first element of the list and does not remove the element. However, it gives a `NoSuchElementException` exception when the list is empty.

getLast()

The `getLast()` method returns the last element of the list and does not remove the element. It gives a `NoSuchElementException` exception when the list is empty.

For a complete list of all the `LinkedList` methods available in Java, check out this page
https://docs.oracle.com/javase/8/docs/api/java/util/LinkedList.html

9.6 Using Lists in our Methods

Now that we are familiar with two of the most commonly used lists in Java, let us look at how we can use these lists in our methods. Using lists in our methods is very similar to how we use arrays in our methods. In the examples below, we'll use an `ArrayList` of `Integer` objects to demonstrate. The same syntax applies for other types of collections.

To accept an `ArrayList<Integer>` as a parameter, we declare the method as

```
public void methodOne(ArrayList<Integer> m)
{
    //Some implementation code
}
```

To return an `ArrayList<Integer>` from a method, we declare the method as

```
public ArrayList<Integer> methodTwo()
{
    ArrayList<Integer> a = new ArrayList<>();
    //Some implementation code

    return a;
}
```

Suppose both `methodOne()` and `methodTwo()` are in a class called `MyClass` and

```
MyClass mc = new MyClass();
```

To call `methodOne()`, we pass in an `ArrayList` as argument

```
ArrayList<Integer> b = new ArrayList<>();
```

```
mc.methodOne(b);
```

To call `methodTwo()`, we assign the result to an `ArrayList`.

```
ArrayList<Integer> c = mc.methodTwo();
```

Chapter 10: File Handling

We've come a long way. By now, you are familiar with quite a few core concepts in Java. In this chapter, we are going to cover another important topic in Java - reading and writing to an external file.

In Chapter 5 previously, we learned how to get input from users using methods like `nextInt()`, `nextDouble()` and `nextLine()` etc. However, in some cases, getting users to enter data into our program may not be practical, especially if our program needs to work with large amounts of data. In cases like this, a more convenient way is to prepare the needed information as an external file and get our programs to read the information from the file.

Java provides us with a number of classes and methods to work with files. The purpose of this chapter is to introduce you to one of the numerous ways to do so. The classes that we are going to look at in this chapter are the `File`, `BufferedReader`, `FileReader`, `BufferedWriter` and `FileWriter` classes. All these classes are available in the `java.io` package. To use the methods in this chapter, you have to add the following import statement:

```
import java.io.*;
```

to your program.

* indicates that we are importing the entire `java.io` package which contains all the classes that we are going to use. Alternatively, you can import the individual classes one by one if you prefer.

10.1 Reading a Text File

To read data from a text file, we use the `FileReader` class. The `FileReader` class reads the contents of a file as a stream of characters, reading in one character at a time.

In theory, this is all that is needed to read from a file. Once you create a `FileReader` object, you are ready to read data from the file. However, in practice, this is not the most efficient way to do it. A more efficient way is to wrap a `BufferedReader` object around the `FileReader` object.

Like the name suggests, a `BufferedReader` object provides buffering for our file reading operation. This concept is similar to video buffering when we view videos online. Instead of reading one character at a time from the network or disk, the `BufferedReader` object reads a larger block at a time so as to speed up the process.

Suppose we want to read data from the file *myFile.txt* located in the same folder as your project. The example below shows how it can be done. To try this example, launch NetBeans and create a new project called *FileHandlingDemo*. Replace the code with the code below:

```
1 package filehandlingdemo;
2 import java.io.*;
3
4 public class FileHandlingDemo {
5
6   public static void main(String[] args) {
7
8       String line;
9       BufferedReader reader = null;
10
11      try
12      {
13          reader = new BufferedReader(new
FileReader("myFile.txt"));
14          line = reader.readLine();
15          while (line != null)
16          {
17              System.out.println(line);
18              line = reader.readLine();
19          }
20      }
```

```
21     catch (IOException e)
22     {
23         System.out.println(e.getMessage());
24     }
25     finally
26     {
27         try
28         {
29             if (reader != null)
30                 reader.close();
31         }
32         catch (IOException e)
33         {
34             System.out.println(e.getMessage());
35         }
36     }
37  }
38 }
```

In the code above, we use a `try-catch-finally` statement to handle our file operations. This is because when working with files, errors can occur. For instance, when we try to open the file, the system may not be able to find the file. This will then generate an error which will be caught in the `catch` block.

Let's look at the `try` block now.

On line 13, we have the following statement:

```
reader = new BufferedReader(new
FileReader("myFile.txt"));
```

Here, we first create a `FileReader` object (the underlined portion) by passing in the path of the file that we want to read. As this file is in the same folder as the project, the path is simply `"myFile.txt"`.

After creating the `FileReader` object, we create a new

BufferedReader object by passing in the FileReader object as an argument to the BufferedReader constructor. This is what we mean when we say "wrap a BufferedReader object around a FileReader object". This is necessary because the BufferedReader object needs to know what data stream to buffer.

After creating the BufferedReader object, we assign it to the variable reader. Now, we are ready to read from the file.

On line 14, we use the readLine() method provided by the BufferedReader class to read the first line in the file. We do that using the statement

```
line = reader.readerLine();
```

If line is not null (i.e. data exists), the while statement from 15 to 19 will be executed. Inside the while statement, we first use the println() method to display the line read onto the screen. We then use another readLine() statement (on line 18) to read the next line. This loop continues running until the last line is read.

Next, from line 21 to 24, we have the catch block. This block simply displays an error message if an exception occurs.

From line 25 to 36, we have the finally block. Inside this block, we use an inner try block (lines 27 to 31) to try closing the BufferedReader object so as to release any system resources that the object might be using. You should always close your BufferedReader object once you no longer need it. If for any reason, we fail to close the object correctly, the inner catch block from line 32 to 35 will catch this error and display the corresponding error message.

That's it. That's how you read a text file in Java. To run this program, first create a text file named *myFile.txt* and save the file in the same folder as the project. If you can't find the project folder, you can right-click on the project name in the Project Explorer in NetBeans and select **Properties**. This will bring up a dialogue box that shows where your project is stored.

You can also save your file somewhere else, but remember to update the path in the program. For instance, if you are using Windows and you saved it in your *Documents* folder, the path will look something like

C:\\Users\\<UserName>\\Documents\\myFile.txt

where <UserName> should be replaced with your own user name. We have to use double slashes \\ when writing this path. This is because if we only use a single slash, the compiler will think the single slash is the beginning of an escape sequence and interpret \U, \D etc as escape sequences. This will result in an error.

Now try running the program. You'll see the content of the text file displayed as output on your screen. Not too complex right?

In fact, there is an even simpler way to read a file in Java. The preceding section is included because there is a lot of legacy code that still uses this old method. However, if you are using Java 7 or beyond, you can use what is known as a `try-with-resources` statement. This statement will automatically close the `BufferedReader` object for us so that we do not have to call the `close()` method explicitly. To try out this method, replace the previous code in the `main()` method with the code below.

```
String line;

try (BufferedReader reader = new BufferedReader(new
FileReader("myFile.txt")))
{
    line = reader.readLine();
    while (line != null)
    {
       System.out.println(line);
       line = reader.readLine();
    }
}
catch (IOException e)
```

```
{
    System.out.println(e.getMessage());
}
```

Notice that we moved the statement

```
BufferedReader reader = new BufferedReader(new
FileReader("myFile.txt"))
```

and placed it within a pair of parenthesis after the `try` keyword? If you do it this way, you do not have to explicitly close the `BufferedReader` object. Java will automatically close the object for us when it is no longer needed. This makes the code much shorter and is also safer as it eliminates the risk of us forgetting to close the object. Try running this new program. It works the same way as the previous program.

10.2 Writing to a Text File

Next, let us look at how to write to a text file. Writing to a file is very similar to reading from it.

To write to a text file, we use the `BufferdWriter` and `FileWriter` class. The code below shows how it can be done. Replace the code in the `main()` method from the example above with the code below.

```
String text = "Hello World";
try (BufferedWriter writer = new BufferedWriter(new
FileWriter("myFile2.txt", true)))
{
    writer.write(text);
    writer.newLine();
}
catch ( IOException e )
{
    System.out.println(e.getMessage());
}
```

Notice that the code above is very similar to the code we wrote when we wanted to read from a file? Indeed, the main difference is that we create a `BufferedWriter` and a `FileWriter` object here instead.

In addition, when we create the `FileWriter` object, we passed in two arguments – the path of the file and the value `true`.

When we create a `FileWriter` object this way, the program will create the file *myFile2.txt* in your project folder if it does not exist. If the file exists, the program will append whatever new data you want to write to the original file (because we indicated `true` for the second argument).

If you want to overwrite any existing data in the file instead, you create a `FileWriter` object like this:

```
new FileWriter("myFile2.txt", false)
```

or like this

```
new FileWriter("myFile2.txt")
```

When the second argument is omitted, the program will overwrite any existing data by default.

Next, after we create the `FileWriter` object, we pass it as an argument to the `BufferedWriter` constructor to create a new `BufferedWriter` object. We then use the `write()` and `newLine()` methods to write to the file.

The `write()` method writes the text to the file. The `newLine()` method moves the cursor to a new line.

Try running this code. If the file *myFile2.txt* does not already exist, a new file will be created in your project folder. Double click on the file created and you'll see the words "Hello World" written on it.

Now run the program again. You'll see a second "Hello World" line added to it.

If you prefer not to append new data, change the statement

```
try (BufferedWriter writer = new BufferedWriter(new
FileWriter("myFile2.txt", true)))
```

to

```
try (BufferedWriter writer = new BufferedWriter(new
FileWriter("myFile2.txt")))
```

Run the program twice and see what happens. When the program is run a second time, only one "Hello World" line is shown on the file. This is because the previous "Hello World" line has been overwritten.

In the example above, we used the `try-with-resources` statement to create our `BufferedWriter` object. Hence, we do not have to explicitly close the `BufferedWriter` object. If you are using a Java version earlier than Java 7, you'll have to close the `BufferedWriter` object in the `finally` block. The way to do it is very similar to what's shown in the first example for this chapter. You can refer to it for help if you are unsure how to do it.

10.3 Renaming and Deleting Files

Now that we know how to read and write to files, let's look at how to rename and delete files in Java. To rename and delete files, we use two pre-written methods found in the `File` class.

To rename a file, we need to create two `File` objects. For instance, if we want to rename *myFile.txt* to *myNewFile.txt*, we create two `File` objects with the two file names as shown below:

```
File f = new File("myFile.txt");
File nf = new File("myNewFile.txt");
```

We can then rename the file by writing

```
f.renameTo(nf);
```

The `renameTo()` method returns `true` if the file is successfully renamed, and `false` if it is not successful.

If you want to delete a file instead, we use the `delete()` method as shown below:

```
nf.delete();
```

This method returns `true` if the file is successfully deleted. Otherwise, it returns `false`.

We'll be using these two methods in your project later.

Chapter 11: Advanced Java Topics

Congratulations! We've come to the last chapter before the project. In this chapter, we are going to briefly cover a few advanced topics in Java, namely: Generics, Lambda Expressions and Functional Interfaces.

11.1 Generics

First, let's look at generics.

We have already used generics when we discussed `LinkedList` and `ArrayList` in Chapter 9. Recall that in Chapter 9, you learned to declare an `ArrayList` of `Integer` using the following statement

```
ArrayList<Integer> myArrayList = new ArrayList();
```

We mentioned that you write `Integer` inside the angle brackets < > to indicate that the `ArrayList` contains `Integer` objects. In contrast, if you want to declare an `ArrayList` of `String` objects, you write

```
ArrayList<String> myArrayList = new ArrayList();
```

This is the gist of generics. Generics allow us to create classes (such as the `ArrayList` class), interfaces and methods in which the type of the data that they operate on is specified as a parameter in angle brackets.

To understand how this works, let's write our own generic class. We'll start with a normal class first.

Launch NetBeans and create a new Project called *GenericsDemo*.

Replace the code with the code below.

```
package genericsdemo;
public class GenericsDemo {
```

```
    public static void main(String[] args) {

        MyGenericsClass g = new MyGenericsClass();

        g.setMyVar(6);
        g.printValue();
    }
}

class MyGenericsClass{

    private Integer myVar;

    void setMyVar (Integer i){
        myVar = i;
    }

    void printValue(){
        System.out.println("The value of myVar is " +
myVar);
    }
}
```

In the code above, we created a class called MyGenericsClass. This class contains a private field (myVar) and two methods called setMyVar() and printValue() which sets and prints the value of myVar respectively.

In the main() method, we instantiated a MyGenericsClass object. Next, we set the value of myVar to 6 and print out its value using the printValue() method. If you run this program, everything will work fine and you'll get the following output:

```
The value of myVar is 6
```

However, let's suppose you want to set the value of myVar to 6.1 instead. Try changing the line

```
g.setMyVar(6);
```

to

```
g.setMyVar(6.1);
```

and run the program again. What happens? You get an error right? This is because `myVar` is declared to be of `Integer` type in `MyGenericsClass`. Since 6.1 is not of `Integer` type, we get an error.

What if you want your class and method to work with both `Integer` and `Double` types? In this case, you can use generics. To do that, you have to make two changes to `MyGenericsClass`.

Firstly, you need to change the class declaration to

```
class MyGenericsClass<T>
```

`T` is known as a type parameter. In other words, it is a parameter for specifying the type of data that the class will operate on. It is a convention to use the uppercase letter T to represent a type parameter.

Next, you need to change all the `Integer` keywords in `myGenericsClass` to `T`.

In other words, you need to change

```
private Integer myVar;
```

to

```
private T myVar;
```

and

```
void setMyVar (Integer i)
```

to

```
void setMyVar (T i)
```

Now try to run the program again. What happens?

The program works now right? In fact, you can set the value of `myVar` to a string and the program will still work. Try changing the line

```
g.setMyVar(6.1);
```

to

```
g.setMyVar("Java");
```

and run the program again. It'll still work.

This, in essence, is how generics work. Generics allow us to create a single class, interface or method that automatically works with different types of data.

Simple enough, right?

However, this is not the sole advantage of using generics. Another advantage of generics is it allows for type-checking.

In our example above, we've just seen that `MyGenericsClass` works with `Integer`, `Double` and `String` type. In fact, it will work with any reference type. While this makes our code more flexible, it can also lead to errors.

For instance, suppose `myVar` is actually used to store the number of students in a class. If there are ten students in the class and we write

```
g.setMyVar(10);
```

all is good. However, suppose we make a mistake and write

```
g.setMyVar(10.2);
```

the compiler will not be able to spot this error since `setMyVar()` is a generic method. This leads to logical errors that can be very difficult to detect in large programs. To overcome this problem, Java provides us with a solution. Instead of declaring g using the statement below,

```
MyGenericsClass g = new MyGenericsClass();
```

we'll be more specific and declare it as follows:

```
MyGenericsClass<Integer> g = new MyGenericsClass();
```

When we add `<Integer>` to the declaration, the compiler will know that the type parameter `T` for `MyGenericsClass` should be replaced with `Integer` when we are working with g.

Hence, if we write

```
g.setMyVar(10.2);
```

we'll get an error.

In short, generics provide us with a way to write classes, interfaces and methods that work with different types of data. Hence, we do not need to write a new class for each data type that we want it to work with.

In addition, when we instantiate an object, we can specify what data type we want the object to work with. This allows the compiler to check for any errors that can arise if we use the wrong data type.

11.1.1 Bounded Types

In the previous section, we discussed how generics work in general. The type parameter `T` in `MyGenericClass` can accept any data type as long as it is a reference type (generics does not work with primitive types).

In this section, we'll look at how we can be more specific when using generics. Sometimes, it may be useful to limit the data types that can be passed to a type parameter. For instance, we may want to create a generic class that only works with numbers. This generic class may contain methods that calculate the sum and average of these numbers. For cases like these, we can use a bounded type parameter. This can be done using the `extends` clause.

If you specify the type parameter as

```
<T extends A>
```

`T` can only accept data types that are subtypes of `A`.

All numeric classes in Java (e.g. `Integer` and `Double`) are subclasses of the `Number` class. If we want our class to only work with numeric data types, we can declare the class as

```
class MyGenericsClass2 <T extends Number>
{

}
```

Now, if we instantiate a `MyGenericsClass2` object as follows,

```
MyGenericsClass2<String> g2 = new MyGenericsClass2();
```

we'll get an error as `String` is not a subclass of `Number`.

In contrast, the statements

```
MyGenericsClass2<Integer> g3 = new
MyGenericsClass2();
MyGenericsClass2<Double> g4 = new MyGenericsClass2();
```

are fine as `Integer` and `Double` are both subclasses of `Number`.

We've just covered a brief introduction of generics. A complete discussion will require a full chapter and is beyond the scope of this book.

Next, let us move on to functional interfaces and lambda expressions.

11.2 Functional Interfaces and Lambda Expressions

The concept of functional interfaces and lambda expressions go hand in hand. First, let's look at the concept of a functional interface.

A functional interface is simply an interface that <u>contains one and only one abstract method</u>. It can contain other static and default methods, but there must only be one abstract method.

Consider the following interface:

```
@FunctionalInterface
interface MyNumber{
    double getValue();
}
```

This interface contains one abstract method (recall that there is no need to use the `abstract` modifier here as methods in interfaces are abstract by default). Since this interface only contains one abstract method, it is known as a functional interface. In a functional interface, the abstract method specifies the intended purpose of the interface. In this example, the function of the interface is to return a certain value that is of `double` type.

You can add the `@FunctionalInterface` annotation to inform the compiler that this is a functional interface as shown in our example above.

Now that we have defined what a functional interface is, let's look at how we can implement this interface. Previously, we learned how we can use a class to implement an interface. In this chapter, we are going to learn how we can use lambda expressions to implement the interface.

The syntax of a lambda expression is as follows

```
(parameter list) -> lambda body
```

This syntax probably looks meaningless at the moment. Let us look at some examples to illustrate how it's used.

Suppose you want to implement the `getValue()` method as follows:

```
double getValue()
{
    return 12.3;
}
```

This method has no parameter and simply returns the value 12.3. We can rewrite the method as the following lambda expression:

```
() -> 12.3;
```

The left side of the lambda expression shows an empty pair of parenthesis which indicates that the method has no parameter. The right side simply consists of the number 12.3. This is equivalent to the statement

```
return 12.3;
```

with the `return` keyword omitted.

Let's look at another example. Suppose you want to implement getValue() as

```
double getValue()
{
    return 2 + 3;
}
```

This method has no parameter and returns the sum of 2 and 3. We can rewrite the method as a lambda expression as shown below:

```
() -> 2 + 3;
```

Next, let's look at a more complex example.

Supposed you want to implement getValue() as

```
double getValue()
{
    int counter = 1;
    int sum = 0;
    while (counter<5)
    {
        sum = sum + counter;
        counter++;
    }

    return sum;
}
```

You can rewrite it as the following lambda expression:

```
() -> {
        int counter = 1;
        int sum = 0;
        while (counter<5)
        {
```

```
        sum = sum + counter;
        counter++;
    }


    return sum;
};
```

Notice that this lambda expression is slightly different from the previous two. Firstly, the lambda body - the right side of the lambda expression - is not made up of a single expression (such as 12.3 and 2+3 in the previous two examples). Instead it contains a `while` statement. The previous two lambda bodies are known as expression bodies because they consist of single expressions. In contrast, the lambda body in the third example is known as a block body.

A block body allows the body of a lambda expression to contain multiple statements. To create a block body, you simply have to enclose the statements in braces as shown in the example above. In addition, you have to add a semi-colon after the closing brace. Finally, as the block body has more than one expression, it is necessary to use the `return` keyword to return a value. This is in contrast to the first two examples where the `return` keyword is omitted.

Now that we are familiar with how lambda expressions with no parameters work, let's look at some examples of lambda expressions that involve parameters. Supposed we have another functional interface called `MyNumberPara` as shown below:

```
@FunctionalInterface
interface MyNumberPara{
    double getValue2(int n, int m);
}
```

This interface has a method called `getValue2()` that has two `int` parameters n and m.

If you want to implement `getValue2()` as:

```
double getValue2(int n, int m)
{
    return n + m;
}
```

We can rewrite the method as the following lambda expression:

```
(n, m) -> n + m;
```

The left side of this lambda expression contains two parameters and the right side shows the expression for computing the return value. It is not necessary for us to explicitly state the data type of the parameters when we use lambda expressions. However, when we invoke the getValue2() method, we must pass in the correct data type. We'll look at how to invoke the getValue2() method later.

Next, supposed we want to implement getValue2() as:

```
double getValue2(int n, int m)
{
    if (n > 10)
        return m;
    else
        return m+1;
}
```

We can rewrite the method as the following lambda expression:

```
(n, m) -> {

        if (n > 10)
            return m;
        else
            return m+1;

    };
```

Now that we are familiar with some basic lambda expressions, let's look at how we can invoke these methods. To invoke these methods, we have to do two things:

First, we need to declare a reference to each of the functional interfaces. We do that by writing

```
MyNumber num1;
MyNumberPara num2;
```

Recall that we cannot instantiate an interface, hence we cannot write something like

```
MyNumber num1 = new MyNumber();
```

but declaring a reference to it is fine.

After declaring the references, we can assign multiple lambda expressions to them.

We'll assign the lambda expressions with no parameter to num1 and the lambda expressions with two parameters to num2.

Following that, we can use num1 and num2 to call the getValue() and getValue2() methods using the dot operator. Let's look at a complete example of how this works.

Launch NetBeans and create a new project called *LambdaDemo*.

Replace the code with the following code:

```
1 package lambdademo;
2
3 public class LambdaDemo {
4
5    public static void main(String[] args) {
```

```
6
7      MyNumber num1;
8
9      num1 = () -> 12.3;
10     System.out.println("The value is " +
num1.getValue());
11
12     num1 = () -> 2 + 3;
13     System.out.println("The value is " +
num1.getValue());
14
15     num1 = () -> {
16         int counter = 1;
17         int sum = 0;
18         while (counter<5)
19         {
20             sum = sum + counter;
21             counter++;
22         }
23
24         return sum;
25     };
26     System.out.println("The value is " +
num1.getValue());
27
28     MyNumberPara num2;
29
30     num2 = (n, m) -> n + m;
31     System.out.println("The value is " +
num2.getValue2(2, 3));
32
33     num2 = (n, m) -> {
34         if (n > 10)
35             return m;
36         else
37             return m+1;
38     };
```

```
39      System.out.println("The value is " +
num2.getValue2(3, 9));
40      //System.out.println("The value is " +
num2.getValue2(3, 9.1));
41   }
42
43 }
44
45 @FunctionalInterface
46 interface MyNumber{
47   double getValue();
48 }
49
50 @FunctionalInterface
51 interface MyNumberPara{
52   double getValue2(int n, int m);
53 }
```

From line 45 to 48, we declared the functional interface `MyNumber`. From line 50 to 53, we declared another functional interface `MyNumberPara`.

From line 5 to 41, we have the `main()` method. Inside the `main()` method, we declare a reference (`num1`) to `MyNumber` on line 7. Next, we assign a lambda expression to `num1` on line 9. On line 10, we invoke the `getValue()` method by writing `num1.getValue()`. We then use the `println()` method to print the value returned by the `getValue()` method.

From line 12 to 26, we include other examples of different lambda expressions and how we invoke the `getValue()` method. From line 28 to 39, we show examples of lambda expressions that take in two `int` arguments. We invoke the `getValue2()` method by passing in two `int` values.

If you run the program above, you'll get the following output:

```
The value is 12.3
```

```
The value is 5.0
The value is 10.0
The value is 5.0
The value is 10.0
```

Note that on line 40, we commented out the statement

```
System.out.println("The value is " +
num2.getValue2(3, 9.1));
```

This is because in this statement, we tried to pass in the values 3 and 9.1 to the `getValue2()` method for `num2`. However, the declaration of `getValue2()` in `MyNumberPara` states that `getValue2()` has two `int` parameters. Hence, we get an error as 9.1 is not of `int` type. Try removing the // in front of this statement and run the program again. You'll get an error.

Chapter 12: Project

Congratulations!! We've come to the last chapter of the book where we'll be working on a project together.

In this final chapter, we are going to get our feet wet by coding a complete console application that demonstrates the different concepts that you just learned.

Ready?

12.1 Overview

For this project, we will be working on a basic membership management program for a fitness centre. This fitness centre has three outlets: Club Mercury, Club Neptune and Club Jupiter. It also has two types of members: Single Club Members and Multi Club Members.

A single club member has access to only one of the three clubs. A multi club member, on the other hand, has access to all three clubs.

The membership fee of a member depends on whether he/she is a single club or a multi club member. For single club members, the fees also depend on which club he/she has access to.

Finally, multi club members are awarded membership points for joining the club. Upon sign up, they are awarded 100 points which they can use to redeem gifts and drinks from the store. Our program will not handle the redemption process. All that we'll do is add 100 points to the multi club member's account.

This application uses a *csv* file to store information about each member. Whenever we launch the application, we'll read the information from the *csv* file and transfer it to a LinkedList. When we add a member to the LinkedList or remove a member from it, we'll update the *csv* file.

Let's start coding our application.

This application consists of six classes and one interface as shown below.

Classes

```
Member
SingleClubMember extends Member
MultiClubMember extends Member
MembershipManagement
FileHandler
Java Project
```

Interface

```
Calculator
```

12.2 The Member Class

We'll start with the `Member` class. This class contains basic information about each member. It serves as a parent class from which two other classes will be derived.

Launch NetBeans and create a new project called *JavaProject*. Add a new class to the `javaproject` **package** and name it `Member`.

Fields

This class has four private fields. The fields are `memberType`, `memberID`, `name` and `fees`, which are of `char`, `int`, `String` and `double` type respectively.

Try declaring the fields yourself.

Constructor

Next, let's create the constructor for the Member class. This class has one constructor with four parameters, pMemberType (char), pMemberID (int), pName (String) and pFees (double). Inside the constructor, we assign the four parameters to the appropriate fields. Try coding this constructor yourself.

Methods

Now, we shall create the setter and getter methods for the four private fields above. All setter and getter methods are public.

Each setter method has an appropriate parameter and assigns the parameter to the field. Each getter method returns the value of the field. An example is shown below:

```
public void setMemberType(char pMemberType)
{
    memberType = pMemberType;
}

public char getMemberType()
{
    return memberType;
}
```

Try coding the remaining setter and getter methods yourself.

Finally, let's write a toString() method for the class. As mentioned earlier in Chapter 8, all classes in Java are derived from a base class known as the Object class. The toString() method is a pre-written method in the Object class that returns a string representing the object. However, the default toString() method is not very informative. Hence, it is customary (and expected of us) to override this method for our own classes.

The method is declared as

```
@Override
public String toString(){

}
```

You are encouraged to add the `@Override` annotation to inform the compiler that you are overriding a method.

This method only does one thing: it returns a string that provides information about a particular member. For instance, the method may return a string with the following information:

```
"S, 1, Yvonne, 950.0"
```

where S, 1, Yvonne and 950.0 are values of the `memberType`, `memberID`, `name` and `fees` fields respectively for this particular member.

Try coding this method yourself.

If you are stuck, you can refer to the example below that shows how you can return a string with the first two fields (`memberType` and `memberID`).

```
return memberType + ", " + memberID;
```

Try modifying this statement to return a string with all the four fields.

Once you are done with this method, the `Member` class is complete.

The list below shows a summary of the `Member` class.

Fields

```
private char memberType;
private int memberID;
```

```
private String name;
private double fees;
```

Constructor

```
Member(char pMemberType, int pMemberID, String pName,
double pFees)
```

Methods

```
public void setMemberType(char pMemberType)
public void setMemberID(int pMemberID)
public void setName(String pName)
public void setFees(double pFees)

public char getMemberType()
public int getMemberID()
public String getName()
public double getFees()

public String toString()
```

12.3 The SingleClubMember Class

Next, we'll code a subclass for the Member class. Add a new class to the javaproject package and name it SingleClubMember.

First, we need to indicate that this class extends the Member class by changing the class declaration to

```
public class SingleClubMember extends Member{

}
```

Fields

The `SingleClubMember` class has one private `int` field called `club`. Try declaring this field yourself.

Constructor

Next, let's code the constructor for the `SingleClubMember` class. This class has one constructor with five parameters, `pMemberType` (`char`), `pMemberID` (`int`), `pName` (`String`), `pFees` (`double`) and `pClub` (`int`). Inside the constructor, we first use the `super` keyword to call the constructor in the parent class. We pass in `pMemberType`, `pMemberID`, `pName` and `pFees` to the parent constructor. Next, we assign the parameter `pClub` to the `club` field.

Try coding this constructor yourself.

Methods

Now, let's add a getter and setter method for the club field. The setter method has an appropriate parameter and assigns the parameter to the field. The getter method returns the value of the field. Both methods are `public`. Try coding these methods yourself.

Finally, we'll code a `toString()` method for this class as well. This method is `public`. It is similar to the `toString()` method in the parent class, but displays an additional piece of information – the club that the member belongs to.

For instance, the method may return a string with the following information:

```
"S, 1, Yvonne, 950.0, 2"
```

where S, 1, Yvonne, 950.0 and 2 are values of the `memberType`, `memberID`, `name`, `fees` and `club` fields respectively.

We can make use of the `toString()` method in the parent class to help us generate the string in the child class.

To use a method in the parent class, we use the `super` keyword just like we did when we called the parent class' constructor. To call the `toString()` method in the parent class, we write

```
super.toString()
```

Recall that this method returns a string? We can then concatenate this string with other substrings to display additional information.

Try coding this method yourself.

Once you are done, the `SingleClubMember` class is complete. The table below shows a summary of the class.

Fields

```
private int club
```

Constructor

```
SingleClubMember(char pMemberType, int pMemberID,
String pName, double pFees, int pClub)
```

Methods

```
public void setClub(int pClub)
public int getClub()

public String toString()
```

12.4 The MultiClubMember Class

Besides the `SingleClubMember` class, we'll also extend another class from the `Member` base class. Add a new class to the *javaproject* package and name it `MultiClubMember`. Use the `extends` keyword to indicate that this class extends the `Member` class.

Fields

The `MultiClubMember` class has one field – a private `int` field called `membershipPoints`. Try declaring this field yourself.

Constructor

Next, code the constructor for the `MultiClubMember` class. This constructor is very similar to the constructor for `SingleClubMember`. It also has 5 parameters. The main difference is the last parameter is `pMembershipPoints` (`int`) instead of `pClub`. Inside the constructor, we'll use the `super` keyword to call the parent constructor. In addition, we'll assign `pMembershipPoints` to the field `membershipPoints`.

Methods

Next, we'll code the getter and setter methods for the `membershipPoints` field. In addition, we'll add a `toString()` method to override the `toString()` method in the parent class. This method prints out the following information:

```
"M, 2, Eric, 1320.0, 100"
```

where M, 2, Eric, 1320.0 and 100 are values of the `memberType`, `memberID`, `name`, `fees` and `membershipPoints` fields respectively.

Try coding these methods yourself. All methods are `public`.

Once you are done, the `MultiClubMember` class is complete. A summary of the class is shown below:

Fields

```
private int membershipPoints
```

Constructor

```
MultiClubMember(char pMemberType, int pMemberID,
String pName, double pFees, int pMembershipPoints)
```

Methods

```
public void setMembershipPoints(int
pMembershipPoints)
public int getMembershipPoints()

public String toString()
```

12.5 The Calculator Interface

Now that we are done with the `Member` class and its subclasses, let us move on to code a functional interface that we'll be using in the project. This interface is a <u>generic</u> interface. You are advised to re-read the previous chapter if you are not familiar with Java generics and functional interfaces.

Create a new Java interface in the *javaproject* package and name it `Calculator`. To do that, right-click on the package name in the Project explorer and select **New > Java Interface**.

This interface only works with numerical data types. Hence, it accepts a bounded type parameter. Try declaring the interface yourself.

Refer to the section on "Bounded Types" in Chapter 11.1.1 if you have forgotten what a bounded type parameter is. The example in that section shows how we declare a generic class. The syntax for declaring a generic interface is similar, except that we use the keyword "interface" instead of "class".

After declaring the interface, we'll add a method to it. The `Calculator` interface is a functional interface and hence only contains one abstract method. This method is called `calculateFees()`. It takes in one parameter called `clubID` and returns a `double` value. Try declaring this method yourself. Once you are done, the interface is complete. A summary for the interface is shown below:

Method

```
double calculateFees(T clubID)
```

12.6 The FileHandler Class

Next, we are ready to move on to code the `FileHandler` class. Add a new class to the *javaproject* package and name this class `FileHandler`.

The class consists of three public methods - `readFile()`, `appendFile()` and `overWriteFile()`.

We need to import the following two packages for the class:

```
import java.util.LinkedList;
import java.io.*;
```

Try importing them yourself.

Methods

readFile()

We shall first code the `readFile()` method. This public method has no parameter and returns a `LinkedList` of `Member` objects. Try declaring this method yourself. You can refer to Chapter 9.6 for help.

Next, let us implement the method. The `readFile()` method reads from a *csv* file that contains the details of each member. It then adds each member to a `LinkedList` and returns the `LinkedList`. The format of the *csv* file is:

Member Type, Member ID, Member Name, Membership Fees, Club ID

for single club members and

Member Type, Member ID, Member Name, Membership Fees, Membership Points

for multi club members.

An example is

```
S, 1, Yvonne, 950.0, 2
M, 2, Sharon, 1200.0, 100
```

For the first row, the values "S", "1", "Yvonne", "950.0" and "2" represent the Member Type, Member ID, Member Name, Membership Fees and Club ID for that particular member. The letter "S" indicates that this member is a single club member.

For the second row, the values "M", "2", "Sharon", "1200.0" and "100" represent the Member Type, Member ID, Member Name, Membership Fees and Membership Points for that particular member. The letter "M" indicates that this member is a multi club member.

The name of the text file is *members.csv* and is stored in the same folder as the project. Hence, the path to the file is simply `"members.csv"` (as it is in the same folder as the project).

Let's start coding the method. We need to declare four local variables as shown below:

```
LinkedList<Member> m = new LinkedList();
String lineRead;
String[] splitLine;
Member mem;
```

After declaring the variables, we'll use a `try-with-resources` statement to create a `BufferedReader` object. We'll name the `BufferedReader` object `reader`.

`reader` accepts a `FileReader` object that reads from *members.csv*. The code for creating a `BufferedReader` object using a `try-with-resources` statement is shown below. You can refer to Chapter 10.1 if you have forgotten what this statement means.

```
try (BufferedReader reader = new BufferedReader(new
FileReader("members.csv")))
{
    //Code inside try block
}
catch (IOException e)
{
    //Code inside catch block
}
```

Within the `try` block, we'll use the `reader.readLine()` method to read the first line of the *csv* file. We'll then assign the result to the local `String` variable `lineRead`. Try coding this statement yourself.

Next, we'll use a `while` statement to process the file line by line while `lineRead` is not `null`.

```
while (lineRead != null)
{
```

```
}
```

Within the `while` statement, we use the `split()` method to split `lineRead` into a `String` array using `", "` as the separator (refer to Chapter 4.1.1). We then assign this result to the local `String` array `splitLine`. Try doing this yourself.

Next, we use the `equals()` method to compare the first element of the `splitLine` array. You can refer to Chapter 4.1.1 if you have forgotten how to use the `equals()` method.

If `splitLine[0]` is equal to `"S"`, we instantiate a `SingleClubMember` object. Else, we instantiate a `MultiClubMember` object. To do that, we use the `if-else` statement below:

```
if (splitLine[0].equals("S"))
{
    //Instantiate a SingleClubMember
}else
{
    //Instantiate a MultiClubMember
}
```

Within the `if` block, we use the constructor for the `SingleClubMember` class to instantiate a new `SingleClubMember` object. We then assign that to the local variable `mem`. As `SingleClubMember` is a subclass of the `Member` class, it is alright for us to assign a `SingleClubMember` object to the `Member` class variable `mem`. The statement for instantiating and assigning a `SingleClubMember` object is shown below:

```
mem = new SingleClubMember('S',
Integer.parseInt(splitLine[1]), splitLine[2],
Double.parseDouble(splitLine[3]),
Integer.parseInt(splitLine[4]));
```

Recall that the constructor for the SingleClubMember class has 5 parameters: `char pMemberType`, `int pMemberID`, `String pName`, `double pFees` and `int pClub`?

As some parameters are of `int` and `double` type while the values in the `splitLine` array are all of `String` type, we have to use the `Integer.parseInt()` and `Double.parseDouble()` methods to parse the `String` values to `int` and `double` values respectively as shown above.

Add the statement above to the `if` block. Once you are done, you can move on to the `else` block.

In the `else` block, we instantiate a `MultiClubMember` object and assign it to `mem`. The constructor of the `MultiClubMember` class has 5 parameters: `char pMemberType`, `int pMemberID`, `String pName`, `double pFees` and `int pMembershipPoints`. Try instantiating a `MultiClubMember` object and assigning it to `mem` yourself.

Once you are done, the `if-else` statement is complete. We can then add `mem` to our `LinkedList` m. The statement below shows how this can be done (refer to Chapter 9.5.1).

```
m.add(mem);
```

Next, we call the `reader.readLine()` method again to read the next line and use it to update the `lineRead` variable.

This is the last step for the `while` statement. You can now exit the `while` statement. Next, exit the `try` block as well. After exiting the `try` block, we'll work on the `catch` block to catch any `IOException` error. This block simply prints out the error. Try coding this `catch` block yourself.

After the `catch` block, we'll return the `LinkedList` m and close the method.

That's all there is to the `readFile()` method. Try coding this method yourself.

appendFile()

Now, let us move on to the `appendFile()` method. This method appends a new line to the *members.csv* file whenever a new member is added. It has a `String` parameter called `mem` and does not return anything. Try declaring the method yourself.

Within the method, we'll use a `try-with-resources` statement to create a <u>BufferedWriter</u> object and name it `writer`. As we want to append to the file instead of overwriting it, we pass the following `FileWriter` object to the `BufferedWriter` constructor:

```
new FileWriter("members.csv", true)
```

Recall that the second argument (`true`) indicates that we want to append to the file.

Try creating the `BufferedWriter` object yourself. You can refer to the previous method for guidance. Creating a `BufferedWriter` object is very similar to creating a `BufferedReader` object, with some slight modifications.

After creating the `BufferedWriter` object, we'll use the `writer.write()` method in the `try` block to append the string `mem` to the *members.csv* file. However, as we want to move the cursor to the next line after we append mem, we'll concatenate `"\n"` to `mem` before passing it as an argument to the `write()` method. In other words, we use the statement below:

```
writer.write(mem + "\n");
```

If we do not do this, we'll end up with

```
S, 1, Yvonne, 950.0, 2M, 2, Sharon, 1200.0, 100
```

instead of

```
S, 1, Yvonne, 950.0, 2
M, 2, Sharon, 1200.0, 100
```

After calling the `write()` method, we can exit the `try` block. Next, we add a `catch` block to catch any `IOException` error. This block simply prints out the error. After the `catch` block, the method is complete. Try coding this method yourself.

overwriteFile()

We are now ready to move on to the `overwriteFile()` method. This method has a `LinkedList<Member>` parameter called `m` and does not return anything. Try declaring the method yourself.

This method is called whenever we want to remove a member from the club. When we remove a member, we need to update our *csv* file. Unfortunately, there is no method in Java that allows us to easily remove a line from a file. We can only write or append to it, but not remove data from it.

Hence, we need to create a temporary file instead. This is a fairly common practice in programming. Here's how it works.

Every time we want to remove a member from our club, we'll remove it from the `LinkedList` first. Next, we'll pass this `LinkedList` as an argument to the `overwriteFile()` method.

Inside the `overwriteFile()` method, we'll create a temporary file called *members.temp* and write all the data in the `LinkedList` to this temporary file. Note that we do not write to the *members.csv* file directly. This is to prevent any error from corrupting the file. If everything goes well, we'll delete the original *members.csv* file and rename *members.temp* to *members.csv*.

In order to achieve what is stated above, we'll first declare a local variable in the `overwriteFile()` method as shown below:

```
String s;
```

Next, we'll use a `try-with-resources` statement to create a `BufferedWriter` object called `writer` and pass the following `FileWriter` object to its constructor.

```
new FileWriter("members.temp", false)
```

Here, we state that we want the `BufferedWriter` object to overwrite any existing data in the *members.temp* file by passing in `false` as the second argument.

Try coding this `try-with-resources` statement yourself.

After creating the `BufferedWriter` object, we can start coding the `try` block. The `try` block starts with a `for` statement as shown below:

```
for (int i=0; i< m.size(); i++)
{

}
```

This `for` statement is used to loop through the elements in the `LinkedList` that is passed in. Inside the `for` statement, we first use the `get()` method to get the element at index `i` (refer to Chapter 9.5.1). We then use the `toString()` method to get a string representation of the element and assign it to the local variable `s`. Recall that we mentioned in Chapter 6.2.3 that you can call two methods in the same statement? We'll do that here to call the `get()` and `toString()` methods in the same statement as shown below:

```
s = m.get(i).toString();
```

Due to polymorphism (refer to Chapter 8.2), the correct `toString()` method will be invoked based on the run time type of the element. For instance, if the first element in the `LinkedList` is a `SingleClubMember` object, the `toString()` method from the `SingleClubMember` class will be invoked.

After getting a string representation of the element, we use the statement

```
writer.write(s + "\n");
```

to write the string `s` to the *members.temp* file.

Once you are done, you can exit the `for` statement and the `try` block.

Next, code a simple `catch` block to catch any `IOException` error and display the error message.

Once you are done, the method is almost complete.

What is left is to delete the original *members.csv* file and rename *members.temp* to *members.csv*. To do that, add a `try-catch` statement after the previous `try-with-resources` statement.

Within the `try` block, we'll declare two `File` objects f and tf as shown below:

```
File f = new File("members.csv");
File tf = new File("members.temp");
```

Next, we'll use the `delete()` method to delete f and use the `renameTo()` method to rename tf. Refer to Chapter 10.3 if you have forgotten how to do this.

Once you are done, you can close the `try` block. The `catch` block that follows simply catches any general exceptions and prints out the error message. Try coding the `catch` block yourself.

After completing the catch block, the `overwriteFile()` method is complete. This is also the end of the `FileHandler` class. We are now ready to code the `MembershipManagement` class. A summary of the `FileHandler` class is shown below:

Methods

```
public LinkedList<Member> readFile()
public void appendFile(String mem)
public void overwriteFile(LinkedList<Member> m)
```

12.7 The MembershipManagement Class

The `MembershipManagement` class is the main focus of the program. This class handles the process of adding and removing members. It also has a method that allows users to display information about a member.

Add a new class to the `javaproject` package and name it `MembershipManagement`.

Next, import the following three packages to our file:

```
import java.util.InputMismatchException;
import java.util.LinkedList;
import java.util.Scanner;
```

We'll first declare a `Scanner` object inside the class and use it to read user input. We'll call the object `reader` and declare it as `final` and `private` as shown below:

```
final private Scanner reader = new
Scanner(System.in);
```

We declare `reader` as `final` because we will not be assigning any new reference to it later in our code. We also declare it as `private` because we'll only be using it in our `MembershipManagement` class.

Next, let us write two private methods. We declare them as `private` because these methods are only needed in the `MembershipManagement` class.

getIntInput()

The first method is called `getIntInput()`. This method is called whenever any method in the `MembershipManagement` class uses the `System.out.println()` statement to prompt users to enter an `int` value. The method tries to read the `int` value entered. If the user fails to enter an `int` value, the method keeps prompting the user to enter a new value until it gets a valid input from the user. It does not have any parameter and returns an `int` value. Try declaring this method yourself.

Within the method, we'll first declare a local `int` variable called `choice` and initialize it to zero. Next, we'll use a `try-catch` statement to try reading in an integer from the user. This `try-catch` statement is placed inside a `while` statement. The `while` statement repeatedly prompts the user to enter an integer as long as the `try` block fails to get a valid value from the user. The `while` statement is shown below:

```
while (choice == 0)
{
    try
    {
      //Code to try reading an integer from the user
    }
    catch (InputMismatchException e)
    {
      //Code to prompt the user to enter a new value
    }
}
```

Within the `try` block, we'll do three things:

First, we'll use the `reader.nextInt()` method to try reading in an integer from the user and assign it to the local variable `choice`.

Next, we want to throw an `InputMismatchException` error if the user enters 0. This is necessary because if the user enters 0, the `while` statement will keep looping. We want the `catch` block to be executed in that case so that the user will be prompted to enter a new value. The `catch` block is where we'll prompt users to enter a new value. To throw an exception, we use the statement below:

```
if (choice == 0)
    throw new InputMismatchException();
```

Refer to Chapter 6.5.2 if you have forgotten what this statement means.

After throwing this exception, the final thing to do is to add a `reader.nextLine()` statement to the `try` block. This is for reading in the newline character that is not consumed by the `nextInt()` method (refer to Chapter 5.4 for more details).

That's all for the `try` block.

After the `try` block, we have a `catch` block that catches an `InputMismatchException` exception. It does two things:

First, it uses `reader.nextLine()` to read in any input that has not been consumed yet. This is necessary because as the `try` block has failed, the input entered by the user has not been fully consumed yet.

Next, the `catch` block displays the following error message to prompt the user to try again.

```
ERROR: INVALID INPUT. Please try again:
```

As long as the code in the `try` block is not executed successfully, the code in the `catch` block will be executed. This means that the value for the local variable `choice` will not be updated as we did not update it in the `catch` block. Hence, the condition

```
choice == 0
```

remains `true` and the `while` statement will keep looping. Only when the user enters a valid integer value will the `while` statement exit.

Once the `while` statement exits, we'll return the value of `choice` and exit the method.

That's all for the `getIntInput()` method. Try coding this method yourself.

printClubOptions()

Next, let us move on to the `printClubOptions()` method. This method is relatively straightforward. It has no parameters and does not return any value. The method simply uses a series of `System.out.println()` statements to print out the following text:

```
1) Club Mercury
2) Club Neptune
3) Club Jupiter
4) Multi Clubs
```

Try coding this method.

getChoice()

Now, we shall code four more methods for this class. All four methods are public methods. The first is a public method called `getChoice()`. It has no parameters and returns an `int` value.

The `getChoice()` method is relatively easy. It has a local `int` variable called `choice` and uses a series of `System.out.println()` or `System.out.print()` statements to print out the following text:

```
WELCOME TO OZONE FITNESS CENTER
=================================
1) Add Member
2) Remove Member
3) Display Member Information

Please select an option (or Enter -1 to quit):
```

Next, it calls the `getIntInput()` method to read the user's input and assigns the user input to the variable `choice`.

Finally, it returns the value of `choice`. Try coding this method yourself.

addMembers()

Now, let us move on to the next public method. This method is called `addMembers()`. It takes in a `LinkedList` of `Member` objects and adds a new member to this `LinkedList`. After adding the member to the `LinkedList`, it returns a string that contains information about the member added.

The method is declared as

```
public String addMembers(LinkedList<Member> m)
{


}
```

and consists of 7 local variables as shown below:

```
String name;
int club;
String mem;
double fees;
int memberID;
Member mbr;
```

```
Calculator<Integer> cal;
```

Note that the last variable is a reference to the `Calculator` interface that we coded earlier.

After declaring the local variables, we are ready to start collecting information about the new member.

Getting the member's name

First, we'll use a `System.out.print()` statement to prompt the user to enter the member's name. We'll then use the `reader.nextLine()` method to read in the input and assign the result to the local variable `name`. Try coding these two statements yourself.

Getting the member's club access

Next, we'll get information about the club(s) that the member has access to.

We'll first call the `printClubOptions()` method. Next, we'll prompt the user to enter the club ID that the member has access to. Finally, we'll use the `getIntInput()` method that we coded earlier to read in the user's choice and assign the value to the local variable `club`.

The valid values for `club` are 1 to 4. Try writing a `while` statement to repeatedly prompt the user to enter the club ID as long as the value entered is not valid. You can refer to the hint below for help:

```
while (club < 1 || club > 4)
{
    //inform user the value is invalid
    //and prompt user to enter new value
    //read the new value and use it to update club
}
```

Calculating the member ID

Now, let us move on to calculate the member ID for the new member. The member ID is an auto-incremented number that is assigned to each new member.

In other words, if the previous member has an ID of 10, the new member will have an ID of 11.

The member ID is calculated using the `if` statement below:

```
if (m.size() > 0)
    memberID = m.getLast().getMemberID() + 1;
else
    memberID = 1;
```

We first check if the `LinkedList` is empty. If it is not, we use the `getLast()` method to get the last element in the `LinkedList`. We then use the `getMemberID()` method that we coded in the `Member` class to get the `memberID` field of that element. Finally, we increase the value by 1 and assign it to `memberID` for the new member.

If the `LinkedList` is empty, the member ID is simply 1. That means the member that we are adding is the first member in the `LinkedList`.

Adding the member to the LinkedList

Now that we have gotten the member's name, club ID and member ID, we are ready to add the member to the `LinkedList` m.

We'll use the following `if-else` statement:

```
if (club != 4)
{
    //Add a single club member
}
else
```

```
{
    //Add a multi club member
}
```

We add a member based on the variable `club`. If the value of `club` is 1, 2 or 3, the member is a single club member. If the value is 4, the member is a multi club member.

Adding a Single Club Member

Let's first look at how we add a single club member. The code for the discussion below should be added to the `if` block of the `if-else` statement above.

We need to first calculate the membership fee of a single club member. To do that, we'll use a lambda expression to implement the `calculateFees()` method in the `Calculator` interface we coded earlier. The method has one parameter – `clubID`.

The club IDs and fees for each club are shown below:

Club Mercury
ID = 1, Fees = 900

Club Neptune
ID = 2, Fees = 950

Club Jupiter
ID = 3, Fees = 1000

The code below shows the implementation of the `calculateFees()` method for a single club member:

```
cal = (n) -> {
    switch (n)
    {
        case 1:
```

```
            return 900;
        case 2:
            return 950;
        case 3:
            return 1000;
        default:
            return -1;
    }
};
```

Here, we use a `switch` statement to implement the method. If the club ID is 1, we return the value 900. If it is 2 or 3, we return the value 950 and 1000 respectively. If it is not 1, 2 or 3, we return the value -1. You can refer to Chapter 11.2 for more information on lambda expressions if you have forgotten how to use them.

After coding this lambda expression, we'll use the statement

```
fees = cal.calculateFees(club);
```

to calculate the membership fee of the single club member and assign it to the variable `fees`.

Next, we'll instantiate a new `SingleClubMember` object by passing in the char value 'S', and the variables `memberID`, `name`, `fees` and `club` to the `SingleClubMember` constructor. We'll then assign this object to the local `Member` variable `mbr` as shown below.

```
mbr = new SingleClubMember('S', memberID, name, fees,
club);
```

After this, we use the `add()` method to add `mbr` to the `LinkedList m`. Try doing this yourself. You can refer to the `readFile()` method in the `FileHandler` class if you have forgotten how to add a member to the `LinkedList`.

After adding the new member, we generate a string representing the new member and assign it to the local variable mem. To do this, we simply use mbr to call the toString() method in the SingleClubMember class. Try coding this statement yourself.

We'll use this String variable to update the *csv* file later.

Finally, we use the statement below to inform the user that the member is added successfully.

```
System.out.println("\nSTATUS: Single Club Member
added\n");
```

This brings us to the end of the if block.

Adding a Multi Club Member

Now, let's work on the else block to add a multi club member to the LinkedList. First, we need to write a new lambda expression to calculate the fee of a multi-club member. This expression should return the value 1200 if the argument passed in is 4. Else, it should return the value -1.

After coding the lambda expression, we'll use it to calculate the fee for a multi club member and assign it to the variable fees.

Next, we'll instantiate a new MultiClubMember object. Recall that the constructor for MultiClubMember has the following 5 parameters: char pMemberType, int pMemberID, String pName, double pFees and int pMembershipPoints?

We'll pass in the char value 'M', the variables memberID, name and fees, and the value 100 to the constructor to create the MultiClubMember object and assign it to mbr.

Next, we'll add mbr to the LinkedList m.

We then generate a string to represent the new member and assign it to mem. Finally, we'll display a message on the screen to inform our user that the new multi club member is added.

Try coding this else block yourself. The else block is very similar to the if block above. You can refer to it for reference.

<u>Returning the value of mem</u>

Once you finish coding the else block, you can close the else block and simply return the value of mem.

With that, you have finished coding the most complex method of the class. Give yourself a pat on the shoulder.

removeMember()

Next, we are ready to move on to the third public method – removeMember(). This method does not return anything. It takes in a LinkedList of Member objects and removes a member from this LinkedList. We'll call this LinkedList m. Try declaring the method yourself.

Within the method, we'll first declare a local int variable called memberID.

Next, we'll prompt the user to enter the Member ID of the member that he/she wants to remove. Next, we use the getIntInput() method to read the input and assign it to the variable memberID. Once that is done, we'll use the for statement below to loop through the LinkedList.

```
for (int i = 0; i<m.size();i++)
{


}
```

Within the `for` statement, we use the `if` statement below to compare the `memberID` of each element with the member ID that the user entered.

```
if (m.get(i).getMemberID() == memberID)
{

}
```

If the member ID matches, we do three things inside the `if` block:

First, we use the `m.remove(i)` method to remove the element at index `i` from the `LinkedList`.

Next, we use a `System.out.println()` statement to inform the user that the member has been removed. Finally, we use the return statement below to exit the method

```
return;
```

We want to exit the method once a matching member ID is found. This is to prevent time wasted on looping through the remaining elements in the `LinkedList`. This example shows how you can use the return statement to exit a method without returning any value from it (refer to Chapter 7.2.2).

Once you are done with the `if` statement, you can close the `if` statement and the `for` statement.

Once we are outside the `for` statement, it means the program has iterated through the entire `LinkedList` and not found a match for the member ID. At this stage, you'll simply use a `System.out.println()` statement to inform the user that the Member ID is not found. Try coding this yourself.

With that, we've come to the end of the `removeMember()` method. We are now ready to code the last public method – `printMemberInfo()`.

printMemberInfo()

This method is very similar to the `removeMember()` method. It also takes in a `LinkedList` of `Member` objects and does not return anything. Try declaring the method yourself.

Within the method, we do the same as what we did for the `removeMember()` method, except that instead of using the `remove()` method to remove a member, we use the `toString()` method to get information about a particular member.

After we have the `String` representation of the member, we use the `split()` method to split this string into a `String` array, using ", " as the separator. The resulting array is then assigned to a local `String` array called `memberInfo`. The statement below shows how this can be done in one step.

```
String[] memberInfo = m.get(i).toString().split(",
");
```

After getting this `String` array, we use it to display information of the requested member using a series of `System.out.println()` statements. If the member is a single club member, the information displayed should look like what is shown below:

```
Member Type = S
Member ID = 1
Member Name = Yvonne
Membership Fees = 950.0
Club ID = 2
```

If the member is a multi club member, the information displayed should look as follows:

```
Member Type = M
Member ID = 2
```

```
Member Name = Sharon
Membership Fees = 1200.0
Membership Points = 100
```

You'll need to use an if statement to test whether the member is a single club member or a multi club member. You can refer to readFile() method in the FileHandler class if you do not know how to do this.

Try modifying the previous removeMember() method and code the printMemberInfo() method yourself.

Once you are done with that, we've come to the end of the MembershipManagement class. We are now ready to work on the final class – the JavaProject class.

A summary of the MembershipManagement class is shown below:

Fields

```
final private Scanner reader
```

Methods

```
private int getIntInput()
private void printClubOptions()
public int getChoice()
public String addMembers(LinkedList<Member> m)
public void removeMember(LinkedList<Member> m)
public void printMemberInfo(LinkedList<Member> m)
```

12.8 The JavaProject class

Switch over to the *JavaProject.java* file to start working on this class. We need to import the LinkedList class. Try importing the class yourself.

The JavaProject class only has one method – the main() method.

We'll use the default declaration for the main() method:

```
public static void main(String[] args) {

}
```

Within the main() method, we have five variables as shown below:

```
String mem;

MembershipManagement mm = new MembershipManagement();
FileHandler fh = new FileHandler();

LinkedList<Member> members = fh.readFile();
int choice = mm.getChoice();
```

The first is a String variable called mem.

Next, we have a MembershipManagement and FileHandler object called mm and fh respectively.

After this, we declare a LinkedList of Member objects. We use the fh object to call the readFile() method in the FileHandler class. This method reads from the *members.csv* file and converts the information into a LinkedList of Member objects. This LinkedList is then returned to the caller. We assign this LinkedList to the local variable members.

Finally, we declare an int variable called choice. We use the mm object to call the getChoice() method in the MembershipManagement class. This method displays a list of options for users to choose and returns the user's choice to the caller. The options are as follows:

```
1) Add Member
2) Remove Member
```

3) Display Member Information

Alternatively, the user can also enter -1 to exit the program.

Once we get the user's choice, we are ready to perform the action that the user wants. To do this, we'll use a `switch` statement inside a `while` statement as shown below:

```
while (choice != -1)
{
    switch (choice)
    {
    }
    choice = mm.getChoice();
}
```

The `while` statement repeatedly prompts the user to enter a choice after each task is completed. For instance, the user may enter 1 for the first time. After we successfully add a member to the `LinkedList`, we'll display the options again and prompt the user to enter another choice (or -1 to exit). As long as the user does not enter -1, the `while` statement will continue to run.

Within the `while` statement, we use a `switch` statement. This `switch` statement consists of 4 cases.

If `choice` is 1, we'll use the `addMembers()` method in the `MembershipManagement` class to add a member to our `LinkedList`. The `addMembers()` method will prompt the user for information about the new member and use that to update the `LinkedList` that we pass in. In addition, it'll return a string that represents the member added. We'll assign this string to the local variable `mem`. Next, we'll use the `appendFile()` method in the `FileHandler` class to add the member to our *members.csv* file. This method does not return any value.

If `choice` is 2, we'll use the `removeMember()` method to remove the member and use the `overwriteFile()` method to update the *csv* file.

If `choice` is 3, we'll use the `printMemberInfo()` method to display the information about the member.

Finally, for the default case, we'll simply notify the user that he/she has selected an invalid option.

Try coding this `switch` statement yourself.

Once you are done with this, our `main()` method is almost complete. We can now exit the `switch` statement. Once we are outside the `switch` statement, we simply use the statement

```
choice = mm.getChoice();
```

to prompt users to select a new option.

After this statement, we can exit the `while` statement. Once we are outside the `while` statement, it means the user has entered -1. Hence, we'll simply print a statement to bid the user good bye. Try coding this statement yourself.

With that, we've come to the end of the `main()` method and the end of the `JavaProject` class.

If you have successfully coded the `main()` program, congratulations! You have just successfully coded a complete program in Java. Well done!

If you have problems coding it, keep trying. You can refer to the suggested solution in Appendix A for reference.

You are now ready to run your program. Excited? Let's do it!

Click on the "Start" button to run the program and key in the values requested.

Try making errors and keying in alphabetical letters instead of numbers. Play around with the program to see how it works. The *members.csv* file is found in the same folder as the project. If you can't find the project folder, you can right-click on the project name in the Project Explorer in NetBeans and select **Properties**. This will bring up a dialogue box that shows where your project is stored.

Does everything work as expected? If it does, great! You have done an excellent job!

If your code does not work, compare it with the sample answer and try to figure out what went wrong. You'll learn a lot by analysing your mistakes. Problem solving is where the fun lies and where the reward is the greatest. Have fun and never give up! The sample answer can be found in Appendix A.

Appendix A

The source code for this program can be downloaded at http://www.learncodingfast.com/java.

Member Class

```java
package javaproject;

public class Member {

    char memberType;
    int memberID;
    String name;
    double fees;

    Member(char pMemberType, int pMemberID, String pName,
    double pFees){

        memberType = pMemberType;
        memberID = pMemberID;
        name = pName;
        fees = pFees;
    }

    public void setMemberType(char pMemberType)
    {
        memberType = pMemberType;
    }

    public char getMemberType()
    {
        return memberType;
    }

    public void setMemberID(int pMemberID)
    {
```

```java
        memberID = pMemberID;
    }

    public int getMemberID()
    {
        return memberID;
    }

    public void setName(String pName)
    {
        name = pName;
    }

    public String getName()
    {
        return name;
    }

    public void setFees(double pFees)
    {
        fees = pFees;
    }

    public double getFees()
    {
        return fees;
    }

    @Override
    public String toString(){
        return memberType + ", " + memberID + ", " + name +
", " + fees;
    }
}
```

SingleClubMember Class

```java
package javaproject;

public class SingleClubMember extends Member{

    private int club;

    SingleClubMember(char pMemberType, int pMemberID,
String pName, double pFees, int pClub){
        super(pMemberType, pMemberID, pName, pFees);
        club = pClub;
    }

    public void setClub(int pClub){
        club = pClub;
    }

    public int getClub(){
        return club;
    }

    @Override
    public String toString(){
        return super.toString() + ", " + club;
    }
}
```

MultiClubMember Class

```java
package javaproject;

public class MultiClubMember extends Member {

    private int membershipPoints;
```

```java
    MultiClubMember(char pMemberType, int pMemberID, String
pName, double pFees, int pMembershipPoints){
        super(pMemberType, pMemberID, pName, pFees);
        membershipPoints = pMembershipPoints;
    }

    public void setMembershipPoints(int pMembershipPoints){
        membershipPoints = pMembershipPoints;
    }

    public int getMembershipPoints()
    {
        return membershipPoints;
    }

    @Override
    public String toString(){
        return super.toString() + ", " + membershipPoints;
    }
}
```

Calculator Interface

```java
package javaproject;

public interface Calculator <T extends Number> {
    double calculateFees(T clubID);
}
```

FileHandler Class

```java
package javaproject;

import java.util.LinkedList;
import java.io.*;

public class FileHandler {
```

```java
public LinkedList<Member> readFile(){
    LinkedList<Member> m = new LinkedList();
    String lineRead;
    String[] splitLine;
    Member mem;

    try (BufferedReader reader = new BufferedReader(new
FileReader("members.csv")))
    {
        lineRead = reader.readLine();
        while (lineRead != null)
        {
            splitLine = lineRead.split(", ");

            if (splitLine[0].equals("S"))
            {
                mem = new SingleClubMember('S',
Integer.parseInt(splitLine[1]), splitLine[2],
Double.parseDouble(splitLine[3]),
Integer.parseInt(splitLine[4]));
            }else
            {
                mem = new MultiClubMember('M',
Integer.parseInt(splitLine[1]), splitLine[2],
Double.parseDouble(splitLine[3]),
Integer.parseInt(splitLine[4]));
            }

            m.add(mem);
            lineRead = reader.readLine();
        }
    }
    catch (IOException e)
    {
        System.out.println(e.getMessage());
    }
```

```java
            return m;
    }


    public void appendFile(String mem){

        try (BufferedWriter writer = new BufferedWriter(new
FileWriter("members.csv", true)))
        {
            writer.write(mem + "\n");
        }
        catch (IOException e)
        {
            System.out.println(e.getMessage());
        }
    }


    public void overwriteFile(LinkedList<Member> m){
        String s;

        try(BufferedWriter writer = new BufferedWriter(new
FileWriter("members.temp", false))){
            for (int i=0; i< m.size(); i++)
            {
                s = m.get(i).toString();
                writer.write(s + "\n");
            }
        }catch(IOException e){
            System.out.println(e.getMessage());
        }

        try{
            File f = new File("members.csv");
            File tf = new File("members.temp");

            f.delete();
            tf.renameTo(f);
        }catch(Exception e){
```

```
                System.out.println(e.getMessage());
        }
    }
}
```

MembershipManagement Class

```java
package javaproject;

import java.util.InputMismatchException;
import java.util.LinkedList;
import java.util.Scanner;

public class MembershipManagement {

    final private Scanner reader = new Scanner(System.in);

    private int getIntInput(){
        int choice = 0;
        while (choice == 0)
        {
            try
            {
            choice = reader.nextInt();
                if (choice == 0)
                    throw new InputMismatchException();
                 reader.nextLine();
            }
            catch (InputMismatchException e)
            {
            reader.nextLine();
                System.out.print("\nERROR: INVALID INPUT.
Please try again: ");
            }
        }
        return choice;
    }
```

```java
    private void printClubOptions(){
        System.out.println("\n1) Club Mercury");
        System.out.println("2) Club Neptune");
        System.out.println("3) Club Jupiter");
        System.out.println("4) Multi Clubs");


    }

    public int getChoice(){
        int choice;

        System.out.println("\nWELCOME TO OZONE FITNESS
CENTER");

System.out.println("=================================");
        System.out.println("1) Add Member");
        System.out.println("2) Remove Member");
        System.out.println("3) Display Member
Information");

        System.out.print("\nPlease select an option (or
Enter -1 to quit): ");
        choice = getIntInput();
        return choice;
    }

    public String addMembers(LinkedList<Member> m)
    {
        String name;
        int club;
        String mem;
        double fees;
        int memberID;
        Member mbr;
        Calculator<Integer> cal;
```

```java
        System.out.print("\nPlease enter the member's name: ");
        name = reader.nextLine();

        printClubOptions();
        System.out.print("\nPlease enter the member's clubID: ");
        club = getIntInput();

        while (club < 1 || club > 4)
        {
            System.out.print("\nInvalid Club ID. Please try again: ");
            club = getIntInput();
        }

        if (m.size() > 0)
            memberID = m.getLast().getMemberID() + 1;
        else
            memberID = 1;

        if (club != 4)
        {
            cal = (n)-> {
                switch (n)
                {
                    case 1:
                        return 900;
                    case 2:
                        return 950;
                    case 3:
                        return 1000;
                    default:
                        return -1;
                }
            };
```

```java
            fees = cal.calculateFees(club);

            mbr = new SingleClubMember('S', memberID, name,
fees, club);
            m.add(mbr);
            mem = mbr.toString();

            System.out.println("\nSTATUS: Single Club
Member added\n");
        }
        else
        {
            cal = (n) -> {

                if (n == 4)
                    return 1200;
                else
                    return -1;
            };

            fees = cal.calculateFees(club);

            mbr = new MultiClubMember('M', memberID, name,
fees, 100);
            m.add(mbr);
            mem = mbr.toString();

            System.out.println("\nSTATUS: Multi Club Member
added\n");
        }
        return mem;
    }

    public void removeMember(LinkedList<Member> m){
        int memberID;

        System.out.print("\nEnter Member ID to remove: ");
```

```java
        memberID = getIntInput();

        for (int i = 0; i<m.size();i++)
        {
            if (m.get(i).getMemberID() == memberID)
            {
                m.remove(i);
                System.out.print("\nMember Removed\n");
                return;
            }

        }
        System.out.println("\nMember ID not found\n");
    }

    public void printMemberInfo(LinkedList<Member> m){

        int memberID;

        System.out.print("\nEnter Member ID to display
information: ");
        memberID = getIntInput();

        for (int i = 0; i<m.size();i++)
        {
            if (m.get(i).getMemberID() == memberID)
            {
                String[] memberInfo =
m.get(i).toString().split(", ");

                System.out.println("\n\nMember Type = " +
memberInfo[0]);
                System.out.println("Member ID = " +
memberInfo[1]);
                System.out.println("Member Name = " +
memberInfo[2]);
                System.out.println("Membership Fees = " +
memberInfo[3]);
```

```java
            if (memberInfo[0].equals("S"))
            {
                System.out.println("Club ID = " +
memberInfo[4]);
            }else
            {
                System.out.println("Membership Points =
" + memberInfo[4]);
            }
            return;
        }
    }
    System.out.println("\nMember ID not found\n");
    }
}
```

JavaProject Class

```java
package javaproject;
import java.util.LinkedList;

public class JavaProject {
    public static void main(String[] args) {

        String mem;

        MembershipManagement mm = new
MembershipManagement();
        FileHandler fh = new FileHandler();

        LinkedList<Member> members = fh.readFile();
        int choice = mm.getChoice();

        while (choice != -1)
        {
```

```java
        switch (choice)
        {
            case 1:
                mem = mm.addMembers(members);
                fh.appendFile(mem);
                break;
            case 2:
                mm.removeMember(members);
                fh.overwriteFile(members);
                break;
            case 3:
                mm.printMemberInfo(members);
                break;
            default:
                System.out.print("\nYou have selected
an invalid option.\n\n");
                break;
        }
        choice = mm.getChoice();
    }
    System.out.println("\nGood Bye");
    }
}
```

Index